WHAT YOUR COLLEAGUES ARE SAYING . . .

This comprehensive resource provides the what, why, and how for effectively implementing small group instruction to support every student! Part A provides excellent suggestions, clearly based in experience, and Part B pairs important content with small group lesson ideas. Such a great resource for ensuring students develop confidence and competence in mathematics!

Jennifer Bay-Williams
Professor and Author, University of Louisville
Louisville, KY

In *Meaningful Small Groups in Math: Meeting All Learners' Needs in Any Setting*, Kimberly Rimbey offers us detailed suggestions on how to get the most out of students working in small groups. These details cover everything from tasks to group size, from how to form the groups to where these groups, once formed, could work. We learn how to answer questions and prompt thinking, and we are provided with detailed lesson plans, planning templates, and resources across a wide range of K–5 mathematics topics. Kimberly Rimbey leaves no stone unturned. I highly recommend this book to any K–5 teacher who is starting to think about using group work as well as any teacher who wants to reexamine and revitalize their use of group work in the classroom.

Peter Liljedahl
Author of *Building Thinking Classrooms in Mathematics Grades K–12*
Professor, Simon Fraser University
Vancouver, BC, Canada

Mathematics is a beautiful, human enterprise and all humans should be given the opportunity to properly experience its wonder and awe, even our society's youngest of humans. We want our students to know, and always believe, that they are genuinely invited to mathematics. Dr. Rimbey's resource shows how.

James Tanton
Global Math Project
Paradise Valley, AZ

We all know that active engagement—*thinking, talking, collaborating, and figuring out*—is the key to learning. We also know that small group, teacher-facilitated work is one way to generate this active engagement. But it's not easy. That's where Dr. Rimbey's wonderfully practical and informative book *Meaningful Small Groups in Math* becomes a powerful resource. With a clear and punchy style—and a slew of examples and models—it's like Kim was your friend and coach talking with you over coffee about what to do, why to do it, and how to do it when it comes to shifting math instruction for the better for all of our students.

Steve Leinwand
Principal Researcher
American Institutes for Research
Washington, DC

As teachers move away from whole class instruction, they are often challenged by exactly what a small group lesson should look like and how to go about planning one. The sample lessons in this book follow math content trajectories across grade levels, with formative assessment ideas to help teachers form their groups. The Explore Before Explain (Eb4E) approach used in the lessons allows students to actively participate in concept development, with the teacher serving as a facilitator. This is a book that should be on your bookshelf!

Donna Boucher
Author and Consultant, Math Coach's Corner
Houston, TX

Small group instruction is such an important part of the learning cycle. Dr. Rimbey breaks down why and then shows teachers, in plain language, how to set up and successfully run teacher-facilitated small groups. She pays extra attention to how different types of groups are used for different instructional purposes and supports teachers in judiciously matching a type of group with a learning need. As if that weren't enough, Dr. Rimbey then breaks down the essential pieces of different elementary mathematics topics and then uses those pieces to show how a particular small grouping strategy elevates that content and makes it more accessible to all students. This book is a must-read for any elementary mathematics teacher or leader.

Paul Gray
President, NCSM: Leadership in Mathematics Education (2021–2023)
Provincetown, MA

Rimbey raises the use of small groups to an art form. Small groups are the mainstay of much of mathematics instruction in the form of collaborative and cooperative groups, yet understanding how to organize and facilitate small groups is not always a part of teacher preparation programs or professional learning experiences. How can we better make these opportunities an ideal way to foster student thinking and reasoning, the sharing of ideas in safe spaces, and the inquiry-oriented approach we prize? *Meaningful Small Groups in Math* guides you through this common configuration. With the wisdom and insight Rimbey gleaned from years of experience, you will find what you need to effectively use small groups. Dig in to find practical approaches, routines, content examples, and ways to make each and every child's voice prominent as they engage in productive ways to showcase their strengths.

Karen Karp
Professor and Author, Johns Hopkins University
Baltimore, MD

With *Meaningful Small Groups in Math*, Dr. Rimbey offers K–5 teachers a versatile approach to teaching small group lessons in a variety of instructional structures. Her approach is practical, clearly described, and focused on effectively building upon students' mathematical strengths with well-planned lessons. As a valuable resource for teachers who want to "let math take the lead," Rimbey includes a *Math Small Group* Standards Trajectory Document that clearly maps out the interrelatedness of the standards in each domain—something I wish had been available when I was teaching. While the first part of the book provides guidance on how to get started with math small group lessons, the second part of the book delves into how to create and teach rigorous, engaging lessons with sample plans. Both beginning and experienced teachers will find this book to be an invaluable guide for teaching math using small group lessons, which to me is an essential instructional strategy for supporting the needs of all students.

Laney Sammons
Author of *Guided Math: A Framework for Mathematics Instruction*
Thetford Center, VT

This book offers a wealth of tips, strategies, and resources for designing effective and engaging small group instruction. You will find the answer to any question you can imagine including how small group instruction benefits students, ways to design small group lessons, thoughts on session duration, discussions of group membership, and even ideas for setting up the classroom to maximize small group instruction. The planning ideas related to some critical K–5 math topics (like counting and cardinality, base-ten addition/subtraction and multiplication/division, and varied fraction and decimal skills) are an added benefit. This is a valuable resource for any teacher interested in beginning, or enhancing, small group instruction in their K–5 classrooms!

Sue O'Connell
Author and Consultant
Millersville, MD

Facilitating small group instruction in our math classrooms can be one of the most challenging goals we set out to accomplish each year, but where do we begin? From the size and type of group to what is happening in small groups, and when it's happening, it can all be overwhelming. *Meaningful Small Groups in Math* thoughtfully unpacks the smaller nuances and questions surrounding small groups and offers the tools teachers need to meet the needs of the students they support.

Graham Fletcher
Math Specialist
Atlanta, GA

Meaningful Small Groups in Math provides teachers with two critical elements for success—practical strategies for managing small groups and thoughtful content trajectories for identifying the right learning for students in small groups. Building on the author's rich classroom and coaching experience, the book provides support for creating and managing small groups in a variety of classroom contexts and structures. And building on the author's deep content knowledge, the book organizes potential activities along content trajectories, helping teachers keep students moving forward in their learning. Dr. Kimberly Rimbey has written an excellent addition to our professional libraries.

Sara Delano Moore
Mathematics Educator & Author
Kent, OH

Kimberly Rimbey's book *Meaningful Small Groups in Math* is a teacher's delight. Rimbey's years of teaching, coaching, and designing come through clearly in every word. Organized around questions teachers would have when considering and implementing math groups—as well as questions teachers may not think to ask but are important—Rimbey writes the book in findable and understandable terms including chapter overviews, learning targets, success criteria—everything we know we should do in a lesson for our own students! Rimbey is an expert at taking the goal of small group learning and showing it in multiple structures that can be integrated with any math program. The practicality of this book is sure to win teachers' hearts.

This book is a must for every elementary math teacher. I applaud Dr. Rimbey's flexibility and multiple examples of using various structures and designs for planning so that there is sure to be a comfortable approach to beginning, extending, or revamping math groups for every teacher!

Nanci Smith
Author & Professor
Glendale, AZ

An essential resource for K–5 mathematics teaching! What a brilliant, practical guide for teachers in using small groups effectively to engage each and every student in powerful mathematics learning! Whether you are just beginning to use small group strategies or you are experienced, there is something for everyone. Rimbey's *Meaningful Small Groups in Math* is a resource for teachers, mathematics coaches, and instructional specialists.

Trena L. Wilkerson
President, National Council of Teachers of Mathematics (NCTM) 2020–2022
Professor of Mathematics Education, Baylor University
Waco, TX

Meaningful Small Groups in Math answers all your burning questions and provides templates and example vignettes that make visualizing this work in your own classroom achievable. Whether you have used small-group instruction extensively, or you are looking to begin, Kimberly Rimbey's *Meaningful Small Groups in Math* gives you exactly what you need . . . and then some! Rimbey masterfully weaves the what, why, when, and—most importantly—the *how* into an easy-to-read book chock full of resources and evidence-based routines.

Hilary Kreisberg
Director, Lesley University's Center for Mathematics Achievement
Author of *Partnering With Parents: A Guide for Teachers and Leaders* (Corwin)
Cambridge, MA

Meaningful Small Groups in Math lays the groundwork for how to create effective mathematics small group instruction. Through vignettes and resources, this book supports your journey to empower student voice and ensure that every child has access to relevant, rich, and meaningful mathematics. This book emphasizes students' assets and shares how to build upon student strengths. You will walk away with practical ideas for how to plan and create teacher-facilitated math small groups to grow students' mathematical understandings.

Mona Toncheff
NCSM Past President (2021–2022)
Pre-Service Teacher Supervisor: University of Arizona
Author and Educational Consultant
Tucson, AZ

Meaningful
Small Groups
in MATH
GRADES K-5

Meaningful Small Groups in MATH

GRADES K-5

Meeting ALL Learners' Needs in Any Setting

Target the Math. . .
Support the Students. . .
Provide Access for All

Kimberly Rimbey

CORWIN Mathematics

FOR INFORMATION:

Corwin

A SAGE Company

2455 Teller Road

Thousand Oaks, California 91320

(800) 233-9936

www.corwin.com

SAGE Publications Ltd.

1 Oliver's Yard

55 City Road

London EC1Y 1SP

United Kingdom

SAGE Publications India Pvt. Ltd.

B 1/I 1 Mohan Cooperative Industrial Area

Mathura Road, New Delhi 110 044

India

SAGE Publications Asia-Pacific Pte. Ltd.

18 Cross Street #10-10/11/12

China Square Central

Singapore 048423

President: Mike Soules

Vice President and
  Editorial Director: Monica Eckman

Publisher: Erin Null

Content Development Editor: Jessica Vidal

Editorial Assistant: Nyle De Leon

Production Editor: Tori Mirsadjadi

Copy Editor: Liann Lech

Typesetter: C&M Digitals (P) Ltd.

Proofreader: Barbara Coster

Indexer: Maria Sosnowski

Cover Designer: Scott Van Atta

Graphic Designer: Gail Buschman

Marketing Manager: Margaret O'Connor

Paperback ISBN 9781071854662

This book is printed on acid-free paper.

22 23 24 25 26 10 9 8 7 6 5 4 3 2 1

CONTENTS

Visit the companion website at
resources.corwin.com/mathsmallgroups
for downloadable resources.

ACKNOWLEDGMENTS

First and foremost, thank you to the teachers with whom I have worked over the years. Your teaching, your questions, your engagement, and your risk taking have helped me learn about teaching mathematics to all students in every setting. This book is dedicated to you—you are the linchpin of our entire education system.

Books are never written in isolation. I am grateful to the team at Corwin for their excellent guidance and expertise. There's a magic in moving from manuscript to book that reminds us of their talents and never ceases to amaze. I also appreciate the input of reviewers and friends who have answered my questions and provided suggestions along the way.

To my friends, colleagues, and mentors who have impacted my heart's work— thank you. Your gracious support, patience, and passion for all things teaching and learning continue to shape me into the educator I am today. To Steve—thank you for believing in me after all these years.

PUBLISHER'S ACKNOWLEDGMENTS

Corwin gratefully acknowledges the contributions of the following individuals:

Katie Basham
K–8 Instructional Coach, Buckeye Elementary School District
Arizona Mathematics Leaders Board Member
Buckeye, AZ

Desiree Yvonne Harrison
Elementary Math Coach, Farmington Public Schools
National Council of Teachers of Mathematics Board Member
Southfield, MI

Penny Roubison
Teacher and Mentor, Empower College Prep
Phoenix, AZ

Chryste Berda
Curriculum Coordinator, Buckeye Elementary School District
Arizona Association of Teachers of Mathematics Board Member
Avondale, AZ

ABOUT THE AUTHOR

Kimberly Rimbey serves as the Chief Learning Officer at KP® Mathematics. A lifelong teacher and learner, her heart's work centers on equipping teachers and helping them fall in love with teaching and learning over and over again. Kim's interests include high-quality professional learning models, building conceptual understanding through multiple representations and meaningful discourse, and building pedagogical content knowledge that goes beyond the theoretical and into the classroom. Always a teacher at heart, Kim has served in many teaching and leadership capacities within school districts, organizations, and the private sector.

Everything Kim has done in her career is based on what she learned during her 18 years as a mathematics coach and elementary classroom teacher. Having started her teaching career as a kindergarten teacher, she frequently says that everything she needed to know about teaching, she learned in kindergarten. Kim is National Board Certified in Early Adolescent Mathematics, and she is a recipient of the Presidential Award for Excellence in Mathematics Teaching. She is the co-inventor of KP® Ten-Frame Tiles and has authored and co-authored several publications, including *Mastering Math Manipulatives* for Corwin, *The Amazing Ten Frame Series* for KP Mathematics, and *Math Power: Simple Solutions for Mastering Math* for the Rodel Foundation of Arizona. Kim earned her BA in Elementary Education and Mathematics from Grand Canyon University, her MEd degrees in Early Childhood Education and Educational Leadership from Arizona State University and Northern Arizona University, and her PhD in Curriculum and Instruction from Arizona State University. She lives in Phoenix, Arizona.

PREFACE

Greetings, my new friend.

If you're reading this book, it means you are looking for ways to meet your students' needs using a small group model. You know your students come to you with strengths, and you're wondering how to organize your time, work, and energy to identify those strengths, build on them, and address opportunities for growth. Your sense of urgency is likely high since you want to do right by these humans sitting in your class. And you might relate to Todd Whitaker when he says that "the best thing about being a teacher is that it matters. The hardest thing about being a teacher is that it matters [every minute] of every day." Meeting the needs of every student every day with the limited time we have is hard work, for sure!

Well, my friend, you're not alone. We're all on this journey to do right by every child every minute of every day. And no matter what your role—classroom teacher, teacher leader, coach, site leader, district leader—we all feel that sense of urgency. My goal in bringing this book to you centers on shedding light on a space that has potential to yield large dividends for the effort—math small group instruction.

Big topics: I'm going to bring forth some hot topics, such as why do reading small groups get so much more attention? What's so destructive about tracking and ability grouping? Why is all this talk about achievement gaps and learning loss both mythical and prevalent? I'm going to challenge your beliefs about your young math learners, because what you believe matters. As you're going through this book, I encourage you to try on some of these ideas for size. Because practice precedes beliefs, and beliefs push practice. What do you believe about your students? What do you believe about their strengths and weaknesses, their math abilities and motivation?

About me: Here's what you need to know about me. I love all things teaching and learning. No matter what role I play professionally, from kindergarten teacher to Chief Learning Officer, I *know* that the linchpin to our entire education system is the classroom teacher. The teacher is the one who has the power to make or break the mathematics experiences our young citizens carry with them for the rest of their lives.

What this book is about: This book is about a powerful approach to small group instruction that targets the math by using math content trajectories. Throughout the book, we'll refer to the small group instruction as teacher-facilitated math small groups, math small groups, or simply small groups. This model helps us support all children in gaining access and connection to grade-level math goals as part of their core instruction in the classroom. It's filled with tools to support you as you support your students. It's intended to work alongside and as part of a variety of math small group structures, Guided Math Workshops, and heterogeneous small groups. My goal in this book is to share how to do teacher-facilitated math small groups in any context, setting up you and your students for ultimate success.

How to interact with this book: Use this as a resource book. You'll likely want to read Part A straight through, though it's well labeled to facilitate skimming. Part B will definitely serve as a day-to-day resource for you. You can jump around through the math content and sample lessons, depending on the math content you're examining, and each chapter in Part B provides a self-standing overview of that topic.

Together, we can do this! Welcome to the journey!

For the kids,

Kimberly Rimbey

Kimberly Rimbey, PhD
National Board-Certified Teacher
Innovator and Encourager

PART A

MATH SMALL GROUP BASICS

HOW TO USE PART A

The first four chapters of this book lay the groundwork for getting started with teacher-facilitated math small groups. Using a question-and-answer format, it provides a user-friendly way for you to find just what you need to get started. You may want to read through all four chapters to familiarize yourself with the approach, or you may simply wish to skim and pull out the most relevant information.

CHAPTER 1

MAKING THE CASE FOR MATH SMALL GROUPS

Learning Intention

After reading this chapter, you will better understand the purpose and benefits for teacher-facilitated math small groups, including how math small groups are similar to and different from reading small groups.

Success Criteria

You will be able to describe the benefits of math small groups, compare and contrast small groups for reading and math, and synthesize your new understandings for how math small groups fit into the broader structure of a mathematics lesson.

CHAPTER INTRODUCTION

Throughout this book, we are going to look at practical ways you can incorporate math small groups into your daily work with students. You may already use a math small group structure that lends itself to small group work in math such as Guided Math, Multi-Tiered Systems of Support, or the math version of "Walk to Read" (sometimes referred to as "What I Need" or WIN Time). Or you may be starting at the very beginning, looking for ways to incorporate small group math instruction into your math program. Either way, the ideas, strategies, frameworks, and helpful tools shared in these pages are intended to enhance the work you're already doing. The overarching, practical questions we will attempt to unravel in this chapter and the next include the following:

1) How do I set up math small groups?
2) What do I do with the students once they're in the small group?
3) What do I do with the rest of the students while I'm working with small groups?

In this first chapter, we take a look at why small group instruction is important in math and begin to lay the foundation for getting started. Then, in Chapter 2, we'll dive into the nuts and bolts for *how* to get started.

WHAT IS THE PURPOSE OF MATH SMALL GROUPS?

If you're like me, I'm sure you are continuously looking for new and better ways to ensure your students maximize their learning during the precious moments you have together. Let's be clear that for the purposes of this book, when we talk about "math small groups," we are talking about teacher-facilitated math small groups. That said, note that "teacher-facilitated" should not be translated as "teacher-facilitated instruction." The purpose of these math small groups is to facilitate student thinking, student discourse, and student discovery. Mathematics cannot be directly transferred from one person to another—it must be investigated and internalized by the students. Therefore, the purpose of math small groups centers on students engaging in rigorous mathematical thinking, facilitated by a teacher who asks purposeful questions to support the students. The student voice should be prominent as they solve problems, engage in tasks, and participate in routines carefully selected to move their thinking forward.

> The purpose of math small groups centers on students engaging in rigorous mathematical thinking, facilitated by a teacher who asks purposeful questions to support the students.

WHY ARE MATH SMALL GROUPS IMPORTANT?

I don't know where I first heard it, but there's a saying that was common among the kindergarten teachers in my district: "We all learn different things on different days in different ways." And to honor such variance, as teachers, we select learning methods and strategies that make learning accessible to each and every child each and every day. Math small groups rise up as one such method. Small groups provide us with a way of ensuring all students have the access and support they individually need to excel in grade-level content and the mathematical practices. They afford teachers the structure needed to support unfinished student learning while connecting to grade-level math goals. They provide students with multiple entry points and multiple ways to express their thinking. Math small groups bring the student to the learning and the learning to the student, accelerating progress in ways unique to each child.

> Math small groups bring the student to the learning and the learning to the student, accelerating progress in ways unique to each child.

Let's take a look at some additional benefits that math small group work provides.

Purposeful Mathematics

During small group instruction, you have the opportunity to ensure that every child has access to relevant, rich, meaningful mathematics. The world around us needs problem solvers, not calculators. We need to humanize mathematics because we now have machines to do what we used to teach kids to do in math—they need to have flexible thinking, reasoning, argumentation, and justification to solve the future problems in the world and be productive citizens. Small group instruction offers you the venue to create a more tailored and personalized way to give students practice in those skills. In the small group setting, all voices can be heard because students can't hide. All students can reveal what they know and ask questions about what they're wondering. You have the opportunity to draw upon students' strengths to help them get where they need to be. And you have the opportunity to help students connect with the purpose of mathematics—to describe and solve problems in the world around them—in personal and relevant ways.

Multiple Modes of Engagement, Representation, and Expression

When using math small groups, you provide a great venue for your students to engage in mathematical thinking in a variety of ways. Universal Design for Learning (CAST, 2018; National Council of Teachers of Mathematics, 2020) suggests that students be provided with multiple modes of engagement, mathematical representation, and action and expression. When we purposefully attend to these modalities while planning for math small groups (and for instruction in general), students gain access to mathematics at entirely new levels. The important work of math is in the thinking, and all learners are capable of engaging in deep and rich thinking given the just-right opportunities. Offering multiple ways of engaging with the math is a matter of access and equity.

> Offering multiple ways of engaging with the math is a matter of access and equity.

Reading Groups Versus Math Groups

Math small groups function differently from reading small groups. In part, this is because "levels" in reading and writing don't work the same way they do in math. Reading is a single process that includes several human-created skills (letter recognition, phonics, decoding, etc.) that must be directly taught for success. In contrast, math uses a variety of concepts that must be explored, discovered, and internalized for success. Granted, skills such as numeral writing, symbols, and vocabulary must be directly taught, but the mathematical sciences must be investigated, discovered, and applied by the individual rather than directly taught from one person to another.

Furthermore, mathematical thinking develops differently from reading foundations skills. Direct instruction—or "I do, we do, you do" teaching—is critical with reading foundations. But with math, we need to offer students multiple ways to engage with math, knowing that they might (and should) represent mathematical concepts or express math ideas in different ways, all of which may be correct. Math small groups provide the just-right avenue for students to pursue multiple pathways that are seen, heard, and validated in ways that facilitate this kind of growth.

Strengths-Based Learning

Talk of learning loss and achievement gaps permeates our world, from the media to the teacher's lounge. Far too frequently, we use these terms broadly to describe the phenomenon of academic disparities within and across student populations. And without realizing it, we buy into a belief that our children are somehow lacking. Rather than focusing on a wide array of strengths that students bring with them, we get caught up in what students "don't have." Math small groups offer us the opportunity to put student strengths at the forefront, building on what they bring to the table. The small group setting provides students with access to meaningful mathematics that impacts them in both school and life. "Sometimes, beliefs about our students' deficits interfere with their access to mathematical ideas. While often well intentioned, when we decide ahead of time that students will likely struggle, we often prevent them from engaging in high-quality instruction" (Kobett & Karp, 2020, p. 101).

> **Strengths-based learning:** a learner-centered approach to teaching and learning where students' strengths are used as a starting point to identify, articulate, and apply individual skills related to what is yet to be learned

Meaningful Supports

Math small groups provide an avenue for us to offer temporary supports that move students' mathematical understandings forward. These supports (tools, structures, processes, etc.) help students think about and make connections to the math goals at hand. Different students require different supports at different times (Hattie et al., 2017, p. 90), and math small groups provide a place where we can work with our students to determine the just-right tools for their toolboxes. In the small group setting, these supports may take the form of facilitated conversations, purposeful questioning, multiple representational opportunities, and the like. Keep in mind that these supports may be used to help students connect current grade-level math goals to unfinished learning from prior grades, incomplete understanding within the current grade, or curiosities about content yet to come in future grades. In other words, *all* children benefit from these supports to connect their mathematical thinking to other math ideas and broader concepts.

WHICH MATH SMALL GROUP STRUCTURE WORKS BEST?

You've probably already figured out that this is a trick question. Teacher-facilitated math small groups come in many different shapes and sizes, and no single structure fits every situation. Depending on the curriculum, resources, and frameworks you use, whether provided by your school system or selected by you, there are many general principles these structures have in common, and you may find yourself wondering about a variety of issues, including group membership selection, time frame and duration, content selection, and how to remain flexible.

Let's take a look at some of these small group structures.

Heterogeneous Math Small Groups

Students are placed into heterogeneously grouped clusters based on conceptual understanding, fluency, rigor level, learning preference, and so on. They may or may not be randomly selected for group membership. The groups usually all work on the same task when they participate in a teacher-facilitated small group.

Homogeneous Math Small Groups

Students are placed into homogeneously grouped clusters based on a specified math skill or concept. This is a very common method of grouping students together because it allows the teacher to focus on the specific skills or concepts that those students need for success. That said, they may also be placed into homogeneous groups based on learning style preference, interest affinities, or the like. The groups usually work on differentiated tasks when they participate in a teacher-facilitated small group.

Guided Math Small Groups

The Guided Math Framework includes a variety of math small group formats, one of which is the teacher-facilitated small group. Students participate in a large group mini lesson and then rotate through math stations or centers with a specified heterogeneous group. The teacher-facilitated small group station is just one of many. The Guided Math Framework typically specifies that students are homogeneously grouped when they go to the teacher-facilitated small group station. Therefore, students are pulled into a homogeneous group to work with the teacher, and then they return to their heterogeneous groups when finished.

Content-Specific Math Small Groups

This is probably the most common type of math small group currently used. Content-specific math small groups typically focus on a single math topic or skill for a specified amount of time (e.g., 1–10 days). Students are assessed and regrouped regularly using any of a variety of formats, such as exit tickets and common formative assessments.

WHEN PENNY PLANS for her math small groups, she typically focuses on the math content currently addressed in the core math program. She wants to be sure all of her students are making progress each and every day. Therefore, she uses the previous day's exit tickets (a single cool-down problem the students solve to show their progress) to determine her math small group assignments for the day. To determine the groups, she sorts the exit tickets into four to five groups based on the temporary supports she wants to offer the students. This content-specific strategy helps her target the math the students need, and it helps her avoid the temptation to put the same students in the same groups day after day, week after week. ●

Math Fluency Small Groups

Many teachers find the need to focus on math fluency in teacher-facilitated small groups. This may include basic math fact fluency, but you may want to move beyond the basics to include opportunities for students to work on the fluency standards as identified by your school system or State Standards Framework. This may include place value, multidigit operations, fractions concepts, fractions operations, and the like. Again, if you are working with out-of-grade-level standards, you will want to strategically connect the small group instruction to current grade-level content.

Number Talks Small Groups

Number Talks typically incorporate the use of mental math strategies as students engage in a small or whole group discussion. The teacher poses a numerical problem and gives the students quiet think time to find a solution. Then students take turns verbally explaining their strategies, often comparing and contrasting their solution paths with those of other students. Number Talks work very well in the small group setting primarily because no one can hide from the conversation and all student voices can be heard. Furthermore, Number Talks can be differentiated for each group. Some teachers even preteach Number Talks with students so they are prepared for whole group Number Talks that take place the next day.

Inquiry-Based Math Small Groups

Inquiry-based math small groups typically focus on solving a given task or problem without up-front instruction. The teacher launches the small group by posing a question and making sure everyone understands it. Then the students set to work using their own solution pathways to find the answer. Many of the previously mentioned small group structures may use an inquiry-based approach while focusing on the selected content.

WHY SHOULD I FOCUS ON STRENGTHS?

For many years, we have focused our efforts on differentiation and intervention (Kobett & Karp, 2020). These structures have contributed a lot to helping us understand how to move students forward in their mathematical understanding.

When done well, these foundational elements of instruction support learners as they fill identified learning gaps. And they also give us the chance to build, massage, and evolve our theories.

More recently, we have come to understand that, when translated into practice, these structures often fall short as they tend to focus more on what the child is missing rather than on the assets that abound inside each child. For example, differentiation tends to be responsive, focused on individual disability, and based on cause and effect. In contrast, Universal Design for Learning tends to be proactive, focused on variability among students, and intentional (CAST, 2018).

By focusing on students' strengths and being intentional in your planning, you can tap into ways you can best support your students. You honor the learning that has already taken place and can build upon and connect to what has come before. By focusing on strengths, you humanize mathematics as you connect children and mathematics. You help them see themselves as people using mathematics to describe and solve problems in the world around them, not simply as calculators looking for correct answers.

> You help them see themselves as people using mathematics
> to describe and solve problems in the world around them,
> not simply as calculators looking for correct answers.

Unfortunately, this is often not the case in a system that urges us to focus on student deficits, learning gaps, and "bubble students." Learning loss and achievement gaps are phenomena used by a large-scale-test-crazy world. These notions describe large-data testing. They do not describe children.

HOW DO MATH SMALL GROUPS FIT INTO A MATH BLOCK SCHEDULE?

Math block schedules differ from school system to school system, so, of course, there is variation for where math small groups will fit into your daily work. The following 90-minute math block will serve as a sample for the sake of this discussion.

- 10–15 minutes: Systematic Review and Preview
- 30–45 minutes: Whole Group Instruction
  - Warm-Up (usually a routine)
  - Launch Task (usually a brief introduction of the task without teacher "show and tell")
  - Explore Task (usually done with partners)
  - Discuss Task (whole-class, student-centered debrief—may include explicit instruction when warranted)
  - Wrap-Up (includes brief formative assessment)

- 30–45 minutes: Math Workshop—may include any mix of the following:
  o Centers or workstations
  o Hands-on activities
  o Teacher-facilitated small groups
  o Student collaboration in pairs or triads
  o Independent practice
  o Application and connections activities
  o Math Circle (10 minutes)—share reflections and make connections

> **Math Workshop:** a framework that allows students to learn new math content, practice math strategies in a variety of ways, and reflect on learning

As you can see in this sample math block, the best time for teacher-facilitated math small groups would be during the Math Workshop time. It's important for you to spend time at the beginning of the year helping your students understand the academic and behavioral expectations when you are occupied with a small group.

WHEN KYANN FIRST started using a teacher-facilitated math small groups model, her goal was to make sure she worked with every student at least once each week. This meant that she needed to keep her math block times tight so that she had enough time to meet with groups every day. Although she longed for a 90-minute math block, she only had 60 minutes to fit in everything.

She got creative with her schedule, and she used 10 minutes at the beginning of the day for students to engage in their systematic math review while she took attendance and attended to other logistics. She had the math problems already posted as the students walked in the door, so they could get right to work, either independently or in pairs. When she finished her morning housekeeping items, she rotated through the room, asking prompting and probing questions to keep students focused, and then led a whole-class conversation that went far beyond the answers—they talked about *how* they solved the problems, *why* they did it that way, and *when* they might use these strategies again.

The beauty of doing this at the beginning of the day was that she could use the data from the review sheets and from her observational notes to help determine group membership for her teacher-facilitated math small groups. In addition, she was also able to see every student in a small group setting at least once per week because of her strategic use of time. ●

WHAT MIGHT A MATH SMALL GROUP SESSION LOOK LIKE?

When you're planning for a math small group session, keep in mind that the focus should be on what the students are going to do, say, and learn. A very good pattern to follow is L-E-D-C: Launch, Explore, Discuss, and Cognitive Closure. At the Center for Recruitment and Retention at the University of Arizona, they frequently frame this process as "Eb4E," or "Explore Before Explain." During a math small group session, this may play out as follows:

- Launch: The teacher poses a question such as a math story or a task.
- Explore: The students work in pairs or individually to find a solution. They represent their thinking using a variety of math tools, engaging in discourse during the exploration. The teacher facilitates the experience with purposeful questions, but does not jump in to show them how to do it. The emphasis is on student thinking.
- Discuss: The teacher facilitates a discussion about what the students just did, making sure that learning was pushed forward. This is the time to engage in a content conversation, if needed.
- Cognitive Closure: The teacher poses a question or problem for the students to answer as they bring the session to a close.

What About Teaching Virtual Math Small Groups?

When teaching students in a virtual environment, not much changes in terms of the Math Small Groups Framework. You still identify strengths and target the math on behalf of all students. And when you create learning pathways, you can still use an Eb4E approach, such as launch-explore-discuss, for planning the session.

What will likely change the most is the use of different representation and presentation apps. If possible, you could provide your students with a manipulatives and math work mats kit to be used during the virtual learning sessions. Although virtual manipulatives serve an excellent purpose and can do some things that physical objects cannot, keep in mind that the virtual objects are really two-dimensional. They are manipulatable, but they cannot replace learning in the 3D world.

When working with physical objects, students can adjust their cameras to show you their work as it happens. This is also true when they are using work mats or writing or sketching on blank paper. When they do so, you can record video or take screenshots to save for portfolios or use for assessment purposes later. You may also want to teach your students how to take and save screenshots of their work to share with others and to submit to you.

YOUR TURN

Throughout this chapter, you had the chance to contemplate how math small groups might look in your context. By considering the structures and schedule, your goals, and how you will identify students' strengths, you lay a foundation for success. Now it's your turn. Take a moment to reflect on the following questions, focusing on how math small groups will benefit the teaching and learning in your classroom.

Learning Intention

After reading this chapter, you will better understand the purpose and benefits for teacher-initiated math small groups, including how math small groups are similar to and different from reading small groups.

Success Criteria

You will be able to describe the benefits of math small groups, compare and contrast small groups for reading and math, and synthesize your new understandings for how math small groups fit into the broader structure of a mathematics lesson.

- How would you describe the benefits for using a math small groups framework in your context?
- Based on what you just read, how might you situate math small groups into your current math instruction?

CHAPTER 2

SETTING UP MATH SMALL GROUPS

> ### Learning Intention
>
> After reading this chapter, you will walk away with practical ideas for how to prepare for and set up teacher-facilitated math small groups.
>
> ### Success Criteria
>
> You will be able to describe how you will set up your classroom for small groups, including the number of students, schedule, duration, and format of your small groups, as well as how you will manage your students, space, and supplies.

CHAPTER INTRODUCTION

In Chapter 2, we continue with our exploration of the three questions posed before Chapter 1:

1) How do I set up math small groups?
2) What do I do with the students once they're in the small group?
3) What do I do with the rest of the students while I'm working with small groups?

In this chapter, we take a look at multiple factors you'll want to consider as you prepare to get your math small groups up and running. We'll discuss group size and the ideal time frame and duration for your small groups. We'll take a look at how to use your teacher-facilitated small group time effectively and how to motivate all children as they enter into the math small group setting. We'll also take a look at how to manage the rest of the class as you work with your math small groups. And, finally, we'll think about how to set up your small group space and what materials you might want to gather in preparation for getting started.

WHAT IS THE IDEAL GROUP SIZE?

Generally speaking, you'll be able to best meet the needs of three to five students at a time. The goal is to make the group sizes small enough so no one can avoid participation! Every student's voice should be heard during this brief time together. During your time with them, take care to invite each student to participate—this is where you can ensure that everyone has a chance to describe their representations and explain their thinking.

When selecting your group size, think about the kind(s) of activities or projects you want students to engage in. Some teachers prefer to include an even number of students in each teacher-facilitated group so that each will have a partner, making two or four the optimal number. If you plan to have students work individually or have the choice to work alone or with a partner, then three or five is fine. Having an odd number of students also facilitates students working in pairs while the teacher works with an individual.

You may find that, on occasion, you want to expand group membership slightly. Groups of five to six students can work, especially with older students, if they are working on a similar task and simply need a nudge. This number also works well when your students are heterogeneously mixed to work on a problem-based task.

WHAT IS THE IDEAL DURATION AND TIME FRAME?

Before we address duration and time frame, remember that group membership should remain *very* flexible. You'll want to take care that you don't place students into small groups that remain unchanged for a long duration and that you aim to focus on just one learning target per small group session. The point is to support each student as they engage in just-in-time strategies that accelerate their learning toward and within grade-level standards.

Duration

Most teachers I have worked with tend to redesign their math small groups about every two weeks. However, your math goal, assessment frequency, and small group structure may lead you to change it up more or less frequently. The important idea here is to keep your group membership flexible so that all students have the opportunity to grow and excel at their unique pace.

To take this a bit further, a math small group might meet for a single day or for several learning episodes, depending on how long it takes to develop the transfer of a skill or concept to application and other situations (Hattie et al., 2017). For some math small groups, you may even find that some students may remain in the group for a longer duration after others "peel off" upon completion of one or two sessions.

NOT TOO LONG ago, Chyste was working on multidigit division in a teacher-facilitated math small group. During their time together, the students were working in pairs as they used manipulatives, sketches, and equations to represent their thinking. Within the first session, it became obvious that some students simply needed a small nudge while others needed deeper work. During session 2, she asked some students to work in pairs as she homed in on one student at a time to detect their thinking. One student peeled off after the second day, another after the third day, and yet another after the fourth.

This left her with just two students, who continued for three more days to dive more deeply into the conceptual work covered in Grades 4 and 5. During this concentrated time, the students were able to accelerate through the prerequisites and then become proficient in their division standards. Using weekly check-ins, Chyste determined that they were maintaining and applying their new understandings within the context of the whole-group Tier 1 instruction. ●

Time Frame

Be sure to keep the focus of each session small, homing in on just *one* grain-sized learning target for each small group. (You may want to use the Math Content Trajectories found in Part B of this book to determine your learning target.)

Here is a general rule of thumb:

- Kindergarten: about 10 minutes for each small group
- Grades 1–2: about 10–15 minutes
- Grades 3–5: about 15–20 minutes

Remember that keeping your groups flexible and fluid is paramount to maintaining a positive experience for all. If you find yourself bringing the same students into the same math small group sessions day after day, week after week, it may be time to rethink your purpose and goals for the group(s). Remember: depending on your goal, you need not work with every student every day and/or every week.

> If you find yourself bringing the same students into the same math small group sessions day after day, week after week, it may be time to rethink your purpose and goals for the group(s).

WHAT SHOULD HAPPEN DURING A MATH SMALL GROUP SESSION?

In order to plan for each teacher-facilitated small group math session, you'll need a lesson plan sequence to help you determine the content you want to cover. You might want to consider a sequence that mirrors the math lesson plan sequence you use for whole group math instruction. Regardless of the small group type you are working with (heterogeneous, content-specific, Guided Math, etc.), the sequence you design should maximize the student voice and minimize your own. Take care to use a sequence that avoids "show-and-tell teaching." Here are a couple of options that might work for you.

Sample Math Small Group Lesson Plan Sequence A

The lesson plan sequence shown in Figure 2.1 aligns well with many textbook lesson plan designs. Each of the four components should align closely with the *single* learning target you've selected for the lesson.

Figure 2.1 · *Sample Lesson Plan Sequence A*

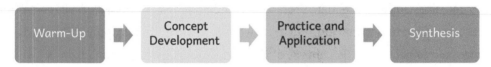

- ▸ **Warm-Up:** This could be a simple game, riddle, intriguing question, or prompt that focuses your students on the selected instructional target. This might also be a *brief* instructional routine such as *Number of the Day* or *Which One Doesn't Belong?* The warm-up should take no longer than three to four minutes.

- ▸ **Concept Development:** Begin by using physical objects or visuals that the students are already familiar with. Get the objects, manipulatives, markers, and so on into the students' hands as quickly as possible, asking them to show and explain how they think about the prompt you provide. Encourage student talk and include context-based problems as much as possible so that students have the opportunity to make sense of the math rather than to simply crunch numbers. The Concept Development and Practice and Application segments should take up the bulk of your time with the students.

- ▸ **Practice and Application:** Ask students to work in pairs and/or individually (determined by your goal ahead of time) to continue showing and explaining their thinking using numbers, pictures, objects, and/or words. Frequently ask prompting and probing questions, and continue to avoid show-and-tell teaching. Avoid overusing paper-and-pencil-based problem sets during this segment. Rather, engage students in group games, partner activities, and the use of whiteboards.

- ▸ **Synthesis:** Ask students a final question about what they worked on today and the progress they made. This is your chance to clear up any misconceptions, ensuring that students leave the group with progress toward the learning target. For example, you might provide sentence stems for students to complete, such as, "What I am beginning to understand about fractions is . . ." "A picture that might show that is . . ." or "The part I'm still trying to understand is . . ." This can also be a place where you co-develop definitions of key vocabulary, create/discuss anchor charts, or preteach content in preparation for the next day's whole group lesson. This segment should always include a check for understanding to help you plan for the next day. The Synthesis segment should take about four to five minutes, depending on the time frame of your lesson.

Sample Math Small Group Lesson Plan Sequence B

The lesson plan sequence shown in Figure 2.2 aligns well with programs that include problem-based learning and inquiry-based strategies. This lesson plan sequence is especially useful if you are working on a problem-based task with heterogeneous groups. As with sample lesson plan sequence A, each of the three components should align closely with the *single* learning target you've selected for the lesson.

Figure 2.2 • *Sample Lesson Plan Sequence B*

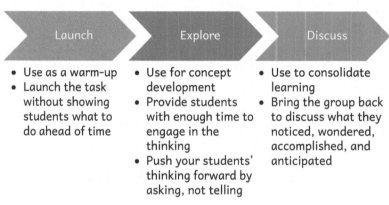

Launch
- Use as a warm-up
- Launch the task without showing students what to do ahead of time

Explore
- Use for concept development
- Provide students with enough time to engage in the thinking
- Push your students' thinking forward by asking, not telling

Discuss
- Use to consolidate learning
- Bring the group back to discuss what they noticed, wondered, accomplished, and anticipated

▶ **Launch:** Begin the session by posing an interesting question or instructing a task prompt that engages students and focuses their attention on the task at hand. Ask prompting and probing questions to ensure your students are on the same page as you. The Launch should take no longer than three to five minutes.

▶ **Explore:** Have students work in pairs or individually, using objects, visuals, and/or equations to show their thinking about the given task. Encourage students to talk with one another, and include context-based problems as much as possible. The Explore segment should take up the bulk of your time with any given small group.

▶ **Discuss/Synthesize:** Use prompting and probing questions to guide students in explaining their reasoning to the rest of the group. Pose strategy questions that lead to reasoning and justification, and encourage students to compare and contrast their solution pathways with others. If you notice any misconceptions, draw those out, again asking prompting and probing questions to center student understanding on the learning target. This can also be a place where you discuss key vocabulary, create/discuss anchor charts, or preteach vocabulary and/or content in preparation for the next day's whole group lesson. This segment should always include a check for understanding to help you plan for the next day. The Discuss/Synthesize segment should take about four to five minutes, depending on the time frame of your lesson.

HOW DO I CHOOSE MY DAILY INSTRUCTIONAL FOCUS?

This will depend, in part, on your selected math small group structure. The first common thread is that you should select a single, grain-sized learning target for each small group session. Second, you should always maintain the goal of supporting students in attaining full understanding of grade-level content.

Create a sequence of daily instructional targets that are connected and sequenced to facilitate deep thinking. Many teachers have found it useful to post the learning targets on a small laminated paper or whiteboard that can be posted for all to see (see Object 2.1).

Object 2.1 • *Sample Daily Instructional Focus Posters*

Let's take a look at how you might go about selecting single daily instructional learning targets.

Heterogeneous Small Group Structure

If your small group structure centers on problem-based tasks or another activity created for heterogeneous groups, then select a just-right, curriculum-aligned task or progression of tasks. Check the rigor level to ensure that the task squarely targets grade-level content.

Homogeneous Small Group Structure

If your small group structure centers on a specific concept or skill with students placed into similar-skill-level groups, then deconstruct the concept or skill into subskills and focus on just one of those learning targets each day. For example, if you are beginning a unit on addition and subtraction strategies, you might make a list of the different strategies your students might use and then sequence them from simple to complex.

The relevant math content trajectories in Part B of this book may help give you a starting point for your analysis. Based on the subskills in your analysis, create exit tickets, common formative assessments, or other tools to determine group membership. Keep in mind that the goal is always to accelerate students toward full and extended understanding of grade-level content as determined by your State Standards Framework. Remember to use the assessments and/or the content trajectories to help you hone a single daily instructional focus for each session.

Guided Math Small Group Structure

If you used the Guided Math structure for math instruction, then you most likely use homogeneous teacher-facilitated groups during your math period. Use your Guided Math assessments—exit tickets (my favorite), common formative assessments, or curriculum-based unit assessments—to determine small group membership. Then use the relevant math content trajectories in Part B of this book to select the just-right rigor level for each group. As with all homogeneous small group structures, keep in mind that the goal is always to accelerate students toward full and extended understanding of grade-level content as determined by your State Standards Framework. Remember to use the assessments and/or the content trajectories to help you hone a single daily instructional focus for each session.

Number Talks, Fluency, or Number Study Structure

If your small group structure depends on a predetermined set of lessons, then you likely already have the daily instructional focus set. That said, most core programs often neglect to break down the content into daily, bite-sized chunks. You may still find the relevant content trajectories in Part B of this book useful in determining the rigor level as you plan for each session. Once you've homed in on your content, create daily instructional focal points for the duration of time that the small group will be meeting.

Content-Specific Structure

If your small group structure focuses on a single concept or skill, keep in mind that, once again, the goal is always to accelerate students toward full understanding of grade-level content. Take care to avoid introducing below-grade-level content without direct connection to the current year's mathematical goals. Again, you will be well served to consult the content trajectories in Part B of this book to determine the just-right rigor level for each small group and then create a series of single-lesson focal points that lead students toward full understanding.

HOW DO I MOTIVATE RELUCTANT STUDENTS?

One of the greatest advantages for using a math small group model emerges from the knowledge that every child wants to feel special and noticed. Because every student gets the chance to spend time with and be heard by the teacher, motivation becomes a natural by-product. Treat each child like a VIP when they come to your group. One way to do this is to reference special interests and hobbies in the context of your discussions.

Students also enjoy thinking deeply about mathematical ideas (Kobett & Karp, 2020). This is especially true when we offer them opportunities that showcase how math is relevant in areas that are of interest to them and that they can relate to. It can be as simple as choosing a rich task to present and changing the context to include the names of your students and the things they enjoy (or detest). Anything to capture their attention will do.

Furthermore, students enjoy learning when choice is involved. This is where Universal Design for Learning (UDL) comes in. How do you plan for various ways for students to engage with, represent, and express their thinking? How do you capitalize on their strengths? How do you set up your small group environment so that it facilitates learning? How intentional are you about embedding these ideas into the small group setting? Some ways you can offer choice might include the following:

- Providing a variety of manipulatives for students within their reach
- Introducing and allowing students to use a variety of visual representations
- Providing a variety of writing tools for students to use to show their thinking
- Frequently asking a variety of prompting and probing questions
- Allowing students to present their thinking in a variety of ways—presentation, poster, visuals, and so on

Each time a small group gathers, you have the opportunity to draw students out of themselves and into the small group community. Here are a few ways to accomplish this:

- Frequently provide students with the opportunity to explain their thinking and reasoning.

- After providing a numerical problem, ask students to create a related context that is customized to them.
- When there is an odd number of students in a group, alternate which student will work directly with you.
- When assigning students to groups for the week (or for a multiweek period), take care that every student has an opportunity to work with you, even if it's just for one session.

And finally, give students something to look forward to. Drop hints about a mysterious task they're going to work on the next day. Find the just-right warm-up routine and promise to use it one day this week. Keep them guessing, and make it playful.

WHAT DOES THE REST OF THE CLASS DO?

This question gets asked more frequently than any other when teachers are contemplating using small group instruction. The question is valid, and it's often based on a belief that students can't or won't work independently without direct, focused supervision. This does not have to be the case, as long as you have set expectations, put self-monitoring strategies in place, and design ways to reinforce the norms. This reinforcement must be extensive at first and then offered periodically throughout the year.

There are many options available for you when deciding how to keep your other students occupied as you work with your students in teacher-facilitated math small groups. Some of the options include the following:

- Set up workstations or learning centers that students might rotate through.
- Put students into cooperative groups to work on a task, activity, or assignment.
- Have students work independently on preassigned work.
- Provide students with a choice card from which they can select their tasks.

Workstations or Learning Centers

Often, teachers set up workstations or learning centers that provide students with specific, focused activities. When you set up your centers, be sure you consider ways in which your students might gain new learning, not simply review current and past content.

There are so many different ways to set up centers. I always like to include the following:

- ▸ Fluency Center
- ▸ Measurement/Geometry Center (connected to current content)

- ▸ Hands-On Center (connected to current lesson)
- ▸ Problem-Solving Center (often filled with puzzles and math-like games)
- ▸ Listening Center (a quiet place to do independent work)
- ▸ Task Card Center (may focus on current content or spiral review)

When setting up centers or workstations, you'll want to consider your space, your management, and your format. Do you want students to stay in the centers for a specified time limit, or do you want them to rotate at their own pace? How many centers will you need for your management purposes? Will centers be located around the room, or will they be portable?

Many math centers books, including those that focus on Guided Math, provide a plethora of options. That work is beyond the scope of this book, but here are a few suggested resources for you to check out:

- ▸ *Figuring Out Fluency in Mathematics Teaching and Learning, K–8* (Bay-Williams & SanGiovanni, 2021)
- ▸ *Guided Math Workshop* (Sammons & Boucher, 2017)
- ▸ *Math Work Stations: Independent Learning You Can Count On, K–2* (Diller, 2011)
- ▸ *Math Workshop in Action: Strategies for Grades K–5* (Newton, 2016b)
- ▸ *Minds on Mathematics: Using Math Workshop to Develop Deep Understanding in Grades 4–8* (Hoffer, 2012)

Independent Small Group or Individual Work

Rather than centers, you may also choose to engage your students in independent or small group work time. In this setting, students work either independently or in cooperative groups as they engage with a game, task, activity, or assignment related to whole group instruction. To minimize disruptions during your teacher-facilitated small groups, you will want to check for understanding with the entire class regarding the instructions and expectations prior to sending them to work cooperatively or independently.

Choice Menu Cards

This technique functions somewhat like learning centers, but instead students can move freely from one activity to the next, based on which choice is selected from the menu. Students may all begin on a common assignment given during whole group instruction. Then, as each student finishes, they select one option from the task card and engage in that activity until it is completed. Similar to the learning centers/workstations, the activities on the choice menu card may include fluency games, task cards, measurement/geometry activities, hands-on tasks, problem-solving activities, independent work, task cards, and the like. Object 2.2 illustrates what a choice card might look like.

Object 2.2 · *Sample Choice Menu Cards*

Menu Card

Choices: Select one or more choices to complete each day. Put an "x" on the day when you complete that choice. At the end of choice time, reflect on what you learned or reinforced each day on the back of this card. Your goal is to complete all nine choices by the end of the week.

Choice 1	Choice 2	Choice 3
Independent Task	Content Game	Fluency Game
M T W Th F	M T W Th F	M T W Th F
Choice 4	**Choice 5**	**Choice 6**
Math and Logic Puzzle	Task Cards	Measurement/Geometry Activity
M T W Th F	M T W Th F	M T W Th F
Choice 7	**Choice 8**	**Choice 9**
Hands-On Activity	Problem-Solving Task	Technology Station
M T W Th F	M T W Th F	M T W Th F

Reflections: What did you discover or reinforce at your choice station(s) today? (Record each day on the back of this card.)

[online resources] **To download this template, visit resources.corwin.com/mathsmallgroups.**

Regardless of which type of system you choose for students to work on while you are not accessible, you will be best served if you establish and practice these routines for several days at the beginning of the school year prior to beginning your teacher-facilitated math small groups. Of course, this leads to considering strategies for minimizing interruptions, which we will talk about next.

ALYSHA'S CLASS BUBBLES with enthusiasm during math workshop every single day. While she works with her teacher-facilitated math small groups, the rest of her students keep busy in the math stations she sets up around the room. She calls her small-group station the "Lifeguard Station," and the rest of the classroom is the "Ocean."

The students in the Ocean rotate through the math stations at their own pace, each keeping track of the work on their individual record sheets. The students in the Ocean currently select from five stations. Note that these stations include work that will push their learning forward, rather than simply engaging them in review and practice.

- The Tier 1 Station, where they complete tasks that push forward learning from today's whole group lesson
- The Tech Station, where they work on a school-adopted adaptive program
- The Math Fluency Station, where they engage in partner math fact games and activities
- The Games Station, where they play games based on strategy and problem solving
- The Task Cards Station, where they complete the task cards Alysha created, usually based on higher-level thinking strategies

Alysha knows that sometimes the students in the Ocean may need additional support while she's working with a math small group. They always check in with three friends first, their life-savers, and that almost always works. However, if they still need support, they can sign in on the board near the Lifeguard Station, knowing that she will check in with them once her teacher-facilitated math small group is finished. ●

HOW DO I MINIMIZE INTERRUPTIONS?

Once you have your system established, continuous reinforcement of student expectations provides the best foundation for minimizing interruptions. The next step includes selecting management techniques that are explicitly taught to students to help them self-monitor as well as let their needs be known. Here are a few to get you started.

- **Teach your routines well and practice on occasion.** Some teachers find it helpful to hold a class meeting at the beginning and/or end of the math block to discuss the management routines, asking students to self-reflect and offer suggestions for making their classroom as learner-friendly as possible.

▸ **Don't start too soon.** As mentioned in the previous section, let students work within your system for several days or a couple of weeks prior to pulling teacher-facilitated small groups so that you can prompt and support independent learning behaviors.

▸ **Set a timer.** Posting a countdown timer for all students to see can help all students pace themselves. It also lets them know when you will once again be available.

▸ **Don't give warnings.** If students choose to disregard expectations while you work with your teacher-facilitated small groups, immediately follow through with predetermined consequences. If you give warnings, the expectations will be treated more like suggestions with some students.

▸ **Establish noise expectations.** Establish and rehearse noise-level expectations up front. Also remind yourself that sometimes the class noise level crescendos naturally, just as the noise level increases in a restaurant as more customers arrive. Anticipate this by creating a visual or audible signal for when the noise level needs to decrease. This can be a simple chime or a quick flicker of the lights. Again, expect immediate response from all students, avoiding the temptation to give warnings.

▸ **Emphasize positive interdependence.** Teach your students to ask for and offer support to one another. The "ask three then me" policy is one example—students should ask three other students for help prior to asking the teacher. This often results in far fewer students needing direct help from the teacher.

▸ **Create a parking lot for questions.** Place a whiteboard or a sheet of chart paper near your small group station where students can post questions and ask for help without interrupting you. When they put their request up, they will see that you have seen their request as you give them a simple glance or a wink. They can then anticipate your support as they watch the timer tick off the minutes until you are once again available.

▸ **Reflect afterwards.** Take a few minutes at the end of your math time to reflect on how well everyone contributed to the learning community. Discuss these routines as well as any others you have implemented, soliciting students' ideas for improving ways in which they can support one another as they learn independently and collectively. With students in younger grades, you may have them sit in a circle on the floor for these discussions. With older students, you may have them put their chairs in a circle. If you use this setup, you have an ideal space for reenacting different situations using a "fishbowl" structure.

Finally, you may want to consider strategically setting students up with "accountability partners" to hold one another accountable during independent or collective learning time. In this case, "strategic" is a key word. When partnering students, consider personality, preference, social skills, and other factors that will set them up for success. The partners may or may not be working on math together. Rather, they act as go-to buddies who can check in from time to time when you are unavailable.

HOW DO I SET UP MY MATH SMALL GROUP SPACE?

Math small groups work best when you have considered how you will organize your physical space and materials. When your space is organized and you have all of your tools at your fingertips, your mind is freed up to focus on instruction and meeting student needs.

Physical Space

Recent trends have shown that expecting students to sit in desks all day does not provide the best environment conducive for learning (Liljedahl, 2021). The recommendations that follow provide you with a variety of options. You may want to consider a space where your teacher-facilitated math small groups might be able to meet in different positions. For example, they might stand for the Launch, work on vertical non-permanent surfaces for the Explore phase, and then sit on the floor for the Discussion. You'll want to explore these options in both your whole-class teaching and your small group teaching.

In *Building Thinking Classrooms in Mathematics, Grades K–12* (2021), Peter Liljedahl uses the phrase "vertical non-permanent surfaces" (or VNPS) to describe mounted whiteboards, or other erasable surfaces, where students can work in small groups on math tasks. These surfaces allow students to easily view other groups' work during the Explore and Discuss phases of learning.

Setting up your small group work space ahead of time will be very beneficial (see Figure 2.3). Be sure you have a designated table and seating for the proper number of students. Additionally, provide a defined workspace for each student at the table. This may include a clipboard for each student's paperwork or a large sheet of craft foam for each pair of students to use as a mat for manipulatives. You will want to include shelves or a cart to organize your math tools on.

Additionally, you will find it very useful to situate yourself so that you can see the whole class as you work with your teacher-facilitated math small groups. And remember to include space for your daily instructional focus board for your small groups as well as the parking lot for the rest of your class to access. Place these in strategic spots so that you and your students can use them with ease.

Figure 2.3 • *Sample Classroom Layout*

Sample Classroom Layout

Vertical surface

Vertical surface

Vertical surface

Vertical surface

Vertical surface

Vertical surface

Vertical surface

Vertical surface

Vertical surface

Vertical surface

Student seating

Student seating

Student seating

Student seating

Student seating

Student seating

Large group floor space

Small group floor space

Teacher has view of entire room

Parking lot

Supplies organized for math small groups

Following are some additional questions for you to consider as you set up your small group work space.

Will Your Students Be Standing Up or Sitting Down?

Most small group areas include tables and chairs where everyone sits for the duration of the session. Although you will likely need this type of seating area at times, you may also want to consider having a small area where the entire group can stand for the Launch, for the closure, or sometimes to work collaboratively through a small group task. Students have been shown to understand and retain the directions for a task longer when the task is delivered orally rather than in writing, and doing this during a stand-up meeting would be optimal (Liljedahl, 2021).

What Type of Writing Surface Will Your Students Use?

Will your students be writing on whiteboards, on paper, in journals, or on vertical surfaces (e.g., whiteboard on the wall)? Be sure you have your writing surfaces and writing tools close by and ready to use. You may want to place baskets of writing tools within student reach. Check ahead of time to make sure pencils are sharpened and markers are working. You do not want your precious learning time disrupted with pencil sharpening or throwing away dried-up markers.

Here are a few more things to consider regarding writing surfaces:

- If you want your students to use a vertical surface, your small group space should be near a wall with a whiteboard or window. (Yes, students can use dry-erase markers on glass.)
- If you want students to write in math journals, purchase or create them ahead of time.
- If you want your students to write on paper, decide what kind of paper to use. Personally, I prefer blank paper, and lightly lined graph paper is my second choice. Also, consider how you want to store it near your space so you always have a handy supply.
- If your students are using paper, consider the following organizational methods: Where will they place their finished work? Do you want them to place completed papers in folders, on a shelf, or in a basket? Do you want students to use clipboards?

Where Will You Place Your Teacher Supplies?

It is important to be sure that everything you need is at your fingertips. You don't want to begin your group and realize that what you need is across the room. Where are you going to store your teacher supplies? Do you have shelves or a cabinet? Will they be in a bucket? What do you need? Dry-erase markers? Colored pencils? A chart stand or whiteboard? Might you put your supplies on a rolling cart to make them multipurpose? Do you need to include a clock or a timer?

In addition to the listed student materials, you may want to consider gathering materials for yourself as well. Those may include the following:

▸ Chart tablet and easel or whiteboard

▸ Hangers, clothespins, and thumbtacks for displaying anchor charts

▸ Markers, colored pencils, pens

▸ Clipboard with blank paper

▸ Method for collecting student data (spreadsheet with student names, sticky notes, notebook, or however you like to keep anecdotal records)

How Will You Store Student Supplies?

Will small sets of manipulatives be placed in tubs, a toolbox, or a supplies caddy? Is there a specific place in the classroom where those materials will be kept when students aren't using them? Will students need computers or other tech devices? How will you store paper, journals, clipboards, markers, and so on so that students can manage themselves? Will you need headphones?

What About Anchor Charts?

If you create relevant anchor charts during whole group instruction, your math small groups will benefit tremendously from interacting with the same chart. Consider how you might place and store anchor charts so they can be available to you during your teacher-facilitated small groups. You might consider clipping your anchor charts to clothes hangers using clothespins (see Object 2.3). If you place thumbtacks in the walls in strategic locations, the anchor charts can be easily moved from one spot to another for easy access.

Object 2.3 • *Portable Anchor Chart*

Source: Clothes hanger image by Spiderstocki/istock.com; Clothespin image by Bigmouse108/istock.com; Blank paper image by tomograf/istock.com.

What Other Math Tools Will You Want at Your Fingertips?

Using a variety of math tools in your teacher-facilitated math small groups provides essential scaffolding for each student. As much as possible, make a variety of materials available so students can self-select the tools that work best for them. You may consider creating a group Mathematicians Tool Kit by placing a variety of appropriate tools in a plastic bin or toolbox and allowing students to self-select the tools they wish to use.

The suggested materials lists throughout this book are organized using the five modes of representation included in the Lesh Translation Model (Lesh et al., 1987; see Figure 2.4). The five categories in this diagram represent the five ways in which mathematics is typically represented:

- ▶ Concrete (physical) objects
- ▶ Visual (e.g., number lines or bar models)
- ▶ Symbolic (e.g., numerals or operation signs)
- ▶ Verbal (either with talking or writing)
- ▶ Contextual (e.g., word problems or descriptions using quantifiable elements)

This resources list is not comprehensive, though it does provide a wide range of options to consider including in your math small groups space. For specific activities using concrete and virtual manipulatives, check out *Mastering Math Manipulatives* (Moore & Rimbey, 2021).

> For specific activities using concrete and virtual manipulatives, check out *Mastering Math Manipulatives* (Moore & Rimbey, 2021).

Figure 2.4 • *Lesh Translation Model of Representations*

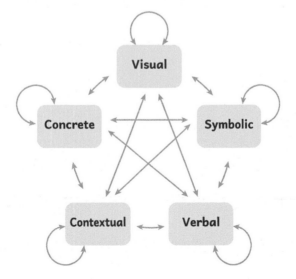

A one-page summary of the following lists can be found on the companion website at resources.corwin.com/mathsmallgroups.

Materials for Concrete Representations

When students use physical objects to represent their thinking, they manipulate the objects in a three-dimensional world. These concrete objects can be helpful in a couple of different ways. First, students can use the manipulatives as communication tools, allowing them to show their thinking as they explain orally. Second, students can use the physical objects as actual thinking tools, discovering new ideas as a result of interacting with the manipulatives.

Some of the concrete objects you might consider stocking on your small group storage shelves are the following:

Math Concept	Manipulatives
Early Number Skills	▸ Counters of any kind, including two-color counters ▸ Unit tiles ▸ Linking cubes

Place Value and Place-Value-Based Operations	▸ Counters of any kind with cups or bands for regrouping
	▸ Unit squares
	▸ Base-ten materials, preferably groupable manipulatives such as
	  • linking cubes,
	  • straws and bands,
	  • counters and containers, and
	  • KP® Ten-Frame Tiles

Fraction and Fraction Operations	▸ Fraction circles ▸ Fraction squares ▸ Fraction tiles/bars ▸ Fraction towers ▸ Cuisenaire® rods ▸ Pattern blocks ▸ Paper and scissors
Measurement	▸ Linking cubes ▸ Unit squares ▸ Nonstandard measurement tools (paper clips, paper strips, etc.) ▸ Standard measurement tools (linear tools such as rulers, weight/mass tools such as balance scales and weights, liquid volume tools such as measuring cups)

(Continued)

(Continued)

Math Concept	Manipulatives
Geometry	▸ Pattern blocks ▸ Tangrams ▸ Geoboards ▸ Unit squares ▸ Unit cubes ▸ Geometric solids

Materials for Visual Representations

In addition to using concrete, physical objects, students can also use visuals such as number lines, number bonds, ten frames, tape diagrams, coordinate grids, and other paper- or screen-based representations to communicate or extend their thinking.

A number of supplies may be used to encourage students to create and interact with visuals during your teacher-facilitated small group sessions, including the following:

▸ Individual whiteboards and dry-erase markers

▸ Vertical writing surfaces and dry-erase markers (e.g., whiteboards on the wall where students can stand and work)

▸ Blank paper and writing utensils

▸ Markers, colored pencils

▸ Graphic organizers, either preprinted or sketched by students; examples include ten frames, part-part-whole charts, place value tables, hundreds boards, number lines, arrays, bar models/tape diagrams, and so on

▸ Clear plastic pockets in which to place the graphic organizers listed above; students can reuse the graphic organizers by placing them in the pockets and writing with dry-erase markers

▸ Laptops for virtual manipulatives apps

> While virtual manipulatives do not replace the power of physical objects in the hands of learners, there are definite advantages to digital tools, particularly when we look at more sophisticated uses of them. For more information about virtual manipulatives, see *Mastering Math Manipulatives: Hands-On and Virtual Activities for Building and Connecting Mathematical Ideas* by Moore and Rimbey (2022).

Materials for Symbolic Representations

Your students may use mathematical symbols to represent their thinking in a variety of ways. Although the most traditional use of symbolic representations is expressions and equations, students may use symbols in very creative ways as well. At the simplest level, your students may use math symbols as labels in their pictures, sketches, and other visuals. Your students may also use symbols to represent any number of nonstandard strategies and processes as they communicate and develop their thinking.

The materials previously mentioned for visual representations are similar to what students need for symbolic representations:

▸ Individual whiteboards and dry-erase markers

▸ Vertical writing surfaces and dry-erase markers

▸ Blank paper and writing utensils

▸ Markers, colored pencils

▸ Online apps

Materials for Verbal Representations

Verbal representations should be a primary tool used in your math small groups. Whether talking or writing, students' voices should dominate in the small group setting. For this category, you'll want to think ahead for how you'll prompt and capture students' verbalizations. Here are a few supplies that might come in handy:

▸ Blank paper and writing tools

▸ Markers

▸ Colored pencils

▸ Writing prompts and sentence starters/sentence frames

▸ Audio recording tools (e.g., audio recorder, smartphone, device with recording capacity)

▸ Online apps for recording written and verbal representations

▸ Magnetic numbers, symbols, letters

Materials for Contextual Representations

Whenever possible, invite students to engage in contextual situations that correspond to the number work they are doing. Although we often think of teacher-created context problems, consider ways you might ask students to engage in creating their own context problems based on numbers or equations you provide.

Again, this category interacts with the previous categories, so almost anything listed for concrete, visual, symbolic, or verbal representations also applies for this category.

HOW DO I DETERMINE GROUP MEMBERSHIP FOR EACH MATH SMALL GROUP?

When it comes to determining group membership for your teacher-facilitated small groups, you must first consider which small group structure you will be using (heterogeneous, content-specific, Guided Math, Number Talk, fluency, etc.). One big question to ask yourself up front is whether you are placing students in homogeneous or heterogeneous groupings. Once you've determined that, you will need to decide on the grouping categories, data sources, and number of topics to be covered.

Grouping Categories, Data Sources, and Assigned Tasks

If you are placing students in homogeneous groups, what criteria will you use to determine group membership? You will most likely be using math proficiency data. However, other possible data sets may include learning style, math representation preference, or language proficiency. Once you've determined your categories, you'll want to consider which data sources will support your grouping decisions. We will look at that in the next section.

If students will be grouped heterogeneously, will you be placing students into randomly selected groups or purposefully selected groups? Randomly selected grouping is simple, as you can use a random name generator (available online) to place students in groups. However, if you are placing students in purposefully selected heterogeneous groups, you will need to consider the criteria you will use to group students and what data sources you will use to determine group placement, just as with the homogeneous groupings.

Once you've determined your categories and your data sources, you'll want to determine the tasks for each small group. Will all groups be working the same tasks, as with heterogeneous groups? Or will each group focus on a different concept or skill, as with Guided Math groups?

Multiple Data Sources

Determining how to place students in teacher-facilitated math small groups is no easy task. As the saying goes, "We are data rich and information poor." We are bombarded with so many data points, test results, and formative assessment observations that it's sometimes difficult to know what to attend to and what should fall into the background. So, what *are* the most useful data to rely on when forming math small groups?

The most public and prominent data we have in front of us include year-end testing data, benchmark assessment data, and grades from the previous year. These data sets are often referred to as "lagging indicators," and they are not the best references when determining instructional goals for students. These data are far too broad, and they are not timely. They can help us discern overall trends, but they tend to be of little use when it comes to identifying learning targets and math goals for our daily work with students (Sammons, 2010).

Furthermore, diagnostic assessments are quite limited in their scope, and again, they are not nuanced enough for us to determine math small group membership when the focus is on grade-level math standards. Further, these diagnostic assessments tend to be too focused on operations and computation, and rarely reflect conceptual understanding of underlying mathematics structures such as place value and properties (Sammons, 2010). They also typically lack error pattern analysis, an important factor in determining the learning pathway for students (Ashlock, 2006). Simply put, diagnostic assessments give us an anemic view of our students' understanding.

> **Diagnostic assessments give us an anemic view of our students' understanding.**

The most useful data to identify students' learning needs for small groups is the data we collect on a daily basis while instructing. For example, you can use teacher-created common formative assessments, math running records (Newton, 2016a), and "just-in-time" assessments such as daily formative assessments and checks for understanding. You might keep anecdotal records that focus on students who are struggling with a concept or skill or who are attempting to connect the current content to something that is yet to be taught. Even simple data collection tools, such as tickets out the door, can help determine which students should be placed in each of your teacher-facilitated math small groups.

> Common formative assessments are created and agreed upon by a group of teachers from the same grade level. The assessments are administered in every class with all students or with a specific group or groups of students in each class. These may include observation checklists, daily exit tickets, weekly quizzes, whiteboard activities, or any number of formative assessment techniques.

Here are some additional options for collecting evidence during the learning process that can then be used to determine group membership for teacher-facilitated math small groups.

▸ **Strategic Observations**: Based on your standards analysis, determine the math concepts/skills you want to observe whether your students can or cannot demonstrate. During whole group instruction, you can use a data collection form (Figure 2.5) to note which students would be best grouped for further study.

Figure 2.5 • *Observation Data Collection Template 1—Whole Group*

Place student names into the left-hand column. Record the targeted math concepts/skills you will be looking for. As students engage in a designated task, record their competency as you see it at a glance.

Student	Math Target 1:	Math Target 2:	Math Target 3:	Notes

Rubric:

- + (successful)
- o (partially successful)
- – (unsuccessful)

To download this template, visit resources.corwin.com/mathsmallgroups.

▶ **Formative Assessment Tasks**: Create formative assessment tasks to evaluate the learning of math content or skills you have identified. These tasks may be given during or after a lesson. You may find it most useful to pose these questions to students as exit tickets at the end of a lesson. One method is to have students solve the problem on slips of paper that can then be sorted into groups after class is over. This sorting task can help you quickly decide which students to place into which groups.

▶ **Common Formative Assessments**: If you and/or your grade level have created common formative assessments, these also might provide insights as to how you might group students.

▶ **Error Analysis**: Not all errors are created equal. Whether you're examining student work, formative assessment solutions, or common formative assessment problems, look beyond the answers to identify *how* students arrived at their solutions. For example, with the problem 356 – 137, a student who subtracts "bottom up" on the ones place (7 – 6 rather than 16 – 7) exhibits an entirely different error than a student who was simply off by one because they counted wrong when subtracting 12 – 7 and recorded a difference of 8 rather than 9.

> For a variety of formative assessment collection tools, check out *Mathematics Formative Assessment: 75 Practical Strategies for Linking Assessment, Instruction, and Learning* (Keeley & Tobey, 2011). Their formative assessment classroom tasks (FACTs) will give you many ways to collect daily just-in-time data from your students.

> For a detailed examination of common error patterns in the elementary grades, check out *Error Patterns in Computation* by Robert Ashlock (2006).

Once your students are in small groups, continue collecting data on their work using either of the other data collection forms in this book, or creating your own data collection system. There are two types of data to collect in this setting. The first focuses on asset-based data. What do your students already know and understand? What is the last thing they knew and understood along the learning pathway you have designed? The second type of data to collect during small group instruction is the progress students make on the identified math concepts or skills.

If you are teaching your teacher-facilitated math small group virtually, data collection may look a little different. Here are some tips for you:

- Collect data while watching students work with a virtual whiteboard application, such as whiteboard.fi or whiteboard.chat.

- Collect data while watching students work with virtual manipulatives. You can view all student screens at sites such as the Math Learning Center (https://www.mathlearningcenter.org/apps) and Braining Camp (https://www.brainingcamp.com/).

- If using devices with movable cameras, such as a laptop with a camera at the top of the screen, students can "fold" the device to make their work visible as they complete it. This is yet another great way to monitor real-time student work, recording your observations as you would if you were making observations in the classroom.

- Pay attention to submitted work, and teach students how to take, save, and submit screenshots.

Math Small Groups Formation

Flexibility and *fluidity* play a major role in forming your teacher-facilitated math small groups. As elementary teachers, we often find it simpler to form small groups for reading than for math. This is in part because of how we use single progress monitoring assessments and/or running records to assist in determining reading groupings. However, there is no single assessment to determine mathematics levels. In fact, we can't even think of "levels" in the same way. This is due in part to the notion that there are many different kinds of thinking involved when learning mathematics as opposed to the single, focused process of learning foundational reading skills.

First, let's take a look at what flexible grouping looks like. Newton (2013, p. 43) describes flexible grouping:

- The focus is on the unit of study, and groups are formed based on focus concepts or skills that emerge as important for helping students gain access to the grade-level content.

- The math content targeted depends on the specific domain and standards. All students get challenging work based on the grade-level math goals during core instruction.

- The group members explore and discuss the targeted math content, bringing insights and connections to the grade-level expectations.

- Everyone works on the grade-level goals and big ideas all the time.

- Students are active throughout the small group time.

Always note that your math small groups may be as short as one session or take several sessions, and they can allow students to work in a variety of groupings throughout the week. In the case of content-specific small groups, the membership of a specific math small group may change depending on when students no longer require specific supports that are offered during small group instruction.

For heterogeneous groups, formative assessment also plays a role in determining how to group students. Rather than placing students into leveled groups, we purposefully group them so that they collectively display a variety of thinking and understanding about the topic at hand. This supports them in making sense of each other's thinking, comparing different solution strategies to their own, and leaning into one another's strengths (Dixon et al., 2019). There is no single way to create these groups—you just want to be sure you have a mix of students displaying strong, competent, and emerging understanding in each group, allowing them to both challenge and support one another through dynamic interactions.

CANDACE USES HETEROGENEOUS grouping with her students. Rather than assigning them to groups based on their performance with a specific skill or concept, she places them in random groups each week using an online name selector. As each group joins her, she poses a contextual task, typically related to the current math unit and sometimes integrated with something they are currently reading, and lets them get to work right away. They have access to a variety of math tools, so they are often working side by side with various manipulatives, visuals, and symbols. They are free to pair up or to work individually on the task at hand. Because Candace analyzes data regularly, she knows how to support each student, no matter who they are grouped with. The tasks she chooses are open-ended enough that everyone can engage from different entry points, and she can support them with any number work where they may get stuck or when they are ready to nudge forward. When they discuss their work, everyone has something to share, regardless of skill level, because of the carefully chosen task that allowed students to work at their own levels. ●

For teacher-facilitated math small groups, remember that the purpose is to provide access to the mathematics by connecting these math skills to the current grade-level content. For example, if you are working on fractions with your fifth-grade students, and your observation data indicate that you have four students who have unfinished learning using the area model for multiplication, you'll form a group that may only meet for one or two days to focus on the area model. Note that every time you meet, you will connect the multiplication area model to the fifth-grade fraction work. In addition, you will find a moment during your whole-class time to help everyone connect the area model for multiplication to fifth-grade fractions.

How Do I Set Up the Virtual Space?

If you're teaching virtually, please read through all the questions in this chapter, as you'll want to think about similar things, especially for your teacher supplies. Here are some additional questions for you to think about.

- **How will you meet with your students?** What platform will you be using? Be sure you familiarize yourself with all of the features of that platform ahead of time so there are no surprises. How will you present your live presentations? How will you present your recorded sessions? What presentation mode will you use (online whiteboard, physical clipboard, etc.)?

- **What apps will you use?** Spend some time working with the apps. Will you be using a virtual whiteboard? Will you be using virtual manipulatives? If you are using virtual manipulatives, have you explored the different options? Note that Math Learning Center (free) and Braining Camp (paid) both have options for viewing all your student screens as they work.

- **What physical materials will your students need?** How are you going to provide those materials to them? What supports will you offer your students to ensure they take care of what you offer?

- **How are you going to provide students opportunities to engage with, represent, and express their thinking using a variety of modalities?** Will your students be sketching? If yes, how will they show their work? Will they be using physical manipulatives? If yes, how will they show their work?

- **How will your students save their work?** Do they know how to take and save screenshots? Do they know how to submit work? Do they know how to take, save, and send photos of their physical work?

YOUR TURN

In this chapter, we focused on many of the variables you'll want to consider as you set up your math small groups. Making purposeful decisions beforehand, such as group size, time frame, duration of instructional focus, physical space, classroom management, and so much more, will facilitate a well-run environment where you and your students can be productive. Now, take a few minutes to reflect on the ways in which you will set up math small groups in your setting.

Learning Intention

After reading this chapter, you will walk away with practical ideas for how to prepare for and set up teacher-facilitated math small groups.

Success Criteria

You will be able to describe how you will set up your classroom for small groups, including the number of students, schedule, duration, and format of your small groups, as well as how you will manage your students, space, and supplies.

- What new ideas or good reminders did you glean from this chapter that will help you optimize your math small groups?
- What are you going to do to prepare for your math small groups?

Consider using Figure 2.6 to guide your preparation.

Figure 2.6 · *Preparation for Teacher-Facilitated Math Small Group Template*

My Ideal Group Size: My Session Time Length: My Ideal Duration (# days):	What will my math small group lesson plan design look like?
What motivation strategies will I use?	What will I do with the rest of my students while I'm meeting with the math small group?
How should I set up my math small group physical space? (sketch your space on the back of this sheet)	What materials will I gather? How will I organize them? ▸ Student Materials: ▸ Teacher Materials:

CHAPTER 3

PLANNING FOR MATH SMALL GROUP INSTRUCTION

> **Learning Intention**
>
> After reading this chapter, you will have a better idea of how to plan for your math small group lessons.
>
> **Success Criteria**
>
> You will be able to plan for all components of your math small group lessons using one of the sample math small group lesson plan sequences or a sequence of your choice.

CHAPTER INTRODUCTION

So far, we've talked about the *why* and the *what* of teacher-facilitated math small groups. In this third chapter, we will shift into the *how* as we answer questions such as, "How do I avoid show-and-tell teaching?" "How do I plan for the just-right rigor level?" and "How do I use a game as a small group task?" As you read through these how-to suggestions, consider ways in which you might plan for each component of your math small group lesson. Note that we will address the selection of your small group mathematics content in Chapter 4.

The sample lesson plan sequence components shared in Chapter 2 will be referenced frequently in this chapter. Here is a brief overview of those components:

Components for Sample Math Small Groups Lesson Plan Sequence A

- ▸ Warm-Up
- ▸ Concept Development
- ▸ Practice and Application
- ▸ Synthesis

Components for Sample Math Small Groups Lesson Plan Sequence B

- ▸ Launch
- ▸ Explore
- ▸ Discuss

HOW DO I AVOID SHOW-AND-TELL TEACHING?

Show-and-tell teaching dominates in many math classrooms in our schools. You know what this looks like: The teacher shows the students how to do the math, explaining as they go, and the students typically watch as the teacher performs the mathematics. There are two problems with this model. First, it puts students into a passive mode, simply watching and hopefully listening. In some classrooms, the students take notes, but they are still nonparticipants in the performance. Second, we assume that just because students are looking at the teacher, they are listening, thinking, and processing what they are seeing and hearing. Do not be deceived—watching is *not* the same thing as listening, and listening is not the same thing as learning.

Originally promoted to support science instruction, the Eb4E Planning Template is a perfect antidote for show-and-tell teaching. Borrowed from the science education world, Eb4E is an acronym for Explore Before Explain (Brown, 2019). In this approach, students explore the mathematics content *before* an explanation is offered. In a sense, this is upside-down from show-and-tell teaching. Using this approach, you pose a question or share a task or activity with students during the warm-up or launch of the lesson. You say just enough to ensure students understand what they are supposed to do. Then, during the concept development/practice and apply/explore components, you simply rotate through the group, asking prompting and probing questions as needed. Finally, you synthesize the conversation with a series of questions, filling any gaps in understanding that remain.

This format is a direct response to the more traditional direct instruction approach of "I do, you do, we do." Instead, we want to flip that pattern to "You do, we do, I facilitate," or "You, y'all, we." Don't get me wrong—the direct instruction approach does have a role, though that role is better suited for reading foundations and mathematical conventions than for most of what we do in math class. The Eb4E approach lends itself to the thinking nature inherent in inquiry-based learning, which has a much stronger role in mathematics than a direct instruction model.

Thinking back to the sample lesson planning structures shared in Chapter 2, you might be able to see that the Launch-Explore-Discuss structure lends itself particularly well to an Eb4E approach. Figure 3.1 provides some specificity for what each of the components might look like if you use the Launch-Explore-Discuss sequence in the Eb4E approach.

Leinwand (2022) calls this kind of flow "gradual reveal," as opposed to "gradual release." Gradual release has its place in the classroom, but in math groups, he claims, it leads to "show-and-tell teaching and monkey-see-monkey-do behaviors." In math class, the use of gradual release methods, or direct instruction, robs students of the opportunity to think. This approach reduces mathematics to sets of processes and procedures rather than opportunities for

Figure 3.1 · *Use of the Launch-Explore-Discuss Sequence for Eb4E*

Sample Lesson Plan Sequence B

Launch	Explore	Discuss
• Use as a warm-up • Launch the task without showing students what to do ahead of time	• Use for concept development • Provide students with enough time to engage in the thinking • Push your students' thinking forward by asking, not telling	• Use to consolidate learning • Bring the group back to discuss what they noticed, wondered, accomplished, and anticipated

students to solve problems and describe the world around them. The Launch-Explore-Discuss structure helps remedy the issues introduced by a direct-instruction approach. When you use it, you ask the children to think and work first, and then the math is gradually revealed through your prompting and probing questions and group discussions.

HOW DO I PLAN FOR JUST-RIGHT MATH CONTENT?

One of the most frequently asked questions I hear regarding math small group instruction is, how do I structure and plan for math small group instruction? One of the most important answers lies in selecting the just-right math content for your groups. Regardless of your group structure (heterogeneous, Guided Math, content-specific, etc.), knowing the content trajectories within and across grade levels is essential. This means you need to know when to address on-grade-level content directly, tackling every nuance and substandard. And you need to know when to dip down into previous grade-level content or extend into future grade-level content, connecting back to on-grade-level content quickly and frequently.

The Math Content Trajectories found in Part B of this book offer you one pathway to help you focus your small group work on your grade-level standards as well as those that come before and after your grade level. When you prepare for your teacher-facilitated small groups, the planning involves setting learning targets and success criteria as well as planning your sequence of tasks based on your understanding of unfinished learning or curiosities about future learning you've identified with your students. Be sure to include the language from your content standards in your planning and in your verbalized learning goals for the small groups.

In addition, the trajectories can help you identify what your students last understood regarding the math topic at hand. When students say, "I don't get it," "I don't understand," or "I don't know what to do," use your understanding of the current trajectory to find out what the student *does* know. Ask, "What do you understand in here?" "At what point did you get stuck?" or say, "Go ahead and talk me through your thinking. I'll listen and support you if needed." Be sure to record student understandings in your anecdotal records.

> We will unpack how to use the Math Content Trajectories in Chapter 4. For now, you might want to take a peek at one of the trajectories aligned to your grade level. It will give you a good context to consider as you read through the rest of the topics in this chapter.

HOW DO I PLAN FOR MATHEMATICAL RIGOR?

Over the past two decades, mathematical rigor has come to be defined as the level at which a concept is being explored and internalized. Although many people think that rigor means "harder" or "more difficult," rigor in mathematics connotes the merging of three important principles: conceptual development, procedural fluency, and application (see Figure 3.2).

Figure 3.2 · *Components of Mathematical Rigor*

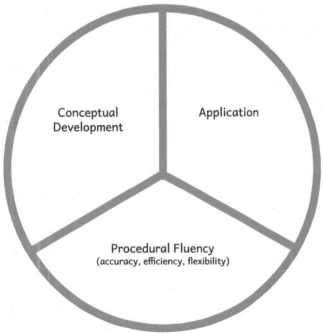

- **Conceptual Development** centers on understanding the underlying mathematical concepts rather than asking students to memorize and apply standard algorithms, methods, and formulas.

- ▸ **Procedural Fluency** includes the skill to carry out mathematical procedures accurately, efficiently, flexibly, and appropriately.
- ▸ **Application** focuses on the ability to apply mathematical ideas to real-world, problem-solving situations.

When you are planning for your math small group sessions, as with any mathematics instruction, you will want to focus on the rigor levels indicated by your objectives, standards, or state/district guiding documents. Typically, grade-level standards specify the rigor level at which students should be working, which can be found in the verbs that are used. This is also something you should attend to as you use the Math Content Trajectories in Part B. Look at the grades in which students are asked to explore concepts, develop fluency, or apply to new situations.

Rigor levels also provide a great starting place for determining how to approach instruction with each of our small groups or even within a small group. I often have students working side by side, with one student representing a concept with manipulatives while their partner represents the same math idea using a procedural fluency method. This benefits both students as they develop an ever-deeper and wider notion of the math concept.

HOW DO I KEEP MY SMALL GROUP MEMBERS ON TRACK?

This certainly can be a challenge! You may find that in the small group setting, students become more talkative and less docile. The setting is somehow less formal, and they feel freer to go off topic, even in the middle of an in-depth academic conversation. This can be annoying at best, and can completely derail the learning at worst.

First, let's focus on being explicit. When we focus our students on the learning goals and explicitly state them up front, we have a much greater chance of being met with success. "Learning intentions can (and often should) have an inherent recursive element in that they build connections between previously learned content and new knowledge" (Hattie et al., 2017, p. 42). Stating the learning intention up front and then revisiting it as necessary may be all some students need.

KATIE EXCELS AT keeping her students on track during her math workshop, including when they work with her during their math small groups. Here's what she knows: *she needs a system for everything.* She spent the first week of school going over all routines and expectations so that there was no question regarding what should be done at any given time. The same was true for her math small groups.

Every day, when the students arrive at the small group table, the learning intention for their group is posted on a whiteboard that sits on a plate stand that Katie bought at the craft store. They read the intention together, and then they go over the task for the day. The foam workmats and writing tools are within reach for every student, and the manipulatives tubs are on a cart at the end of the table, in the event anyone needs them. Students know that their math small group time is precious, and they know that drink and bathroom breaks must be attended to before or after small group. If someone outside the current math small group needs assistance, they know to ask three others for help before approaching the small group area. And even then, they know to simply write their name on the Parking Lot board, never interrupting their classmates' precious learning time.

Because systems and expectations have been so well crafted and communicated, Katie is able to focus on keeping her students' attention on the math, asking prompting and probing questions, and targeting the math for every student in her presence. ●

In addition, Hattie et al. (2017) point out that task selection also makes a difference. When the tasks elicit just the right amount of productive math struggle and keep our students engaged in thinking, they are going to stay on track. Motivation to think is what we're after, right? To determine if a task elicits the "just-right" level of productive math struggle, consider the following prompts included in *Productive Math Struggle* by SanGiovanni et al. (2020) and shown in Figure 3.3.

> More information about the characteristics of a quality math task can be found in *Productive Math Struggle* by SanGiovanni et al. (2020).

Figure 3.3 · *Characteristics of a Quality Math Task*

✓ Aligns to a mathematics content standard I am teaching
✓ Encourages my students to use representations
✓ Provides my students with an opportunity for communicating their reasoning
✓ Has multiple entry points
✓ Allows for different strategies for finding solutions
✓ Makes connections between mathematical concepts, between concepts and procedures, or between application and procedure
✓ Prompts cognitive effort
✓ Is problem-based, authentic, or interesting

Finally, in *Building Thinking Classrooms in Mathematics*, Liljedahl (2021, p. 84) offers us some great advice that can help us keep students on track. He describes three types of questions our students tend to ask when they're supposed to be doing work:

- Proximity questions
- Stop-thinking questions
- Keep-thinking questions

Proximity questions are the ones our students ask just because we're nearby. At face value, they seem innocent enough, but in reality, they're more about conveying the image of a good student rather than truly soliciting support. Often, students ask a question, get an answer, and then don't even do anything with the information they gleaned. And let's face it—during small group instruction, we tend to be completely accessible to them the entire time.

Stop-thinking questions tend to fall into the category of things that annoy us most. "Do we have to learn this?" "Is this going to be on the test?" "Is this right?" These questions are usually motivated by the reality that thinking is hard, and students are trying to offload the thinking onto someone else.

Keep-thinking questions include questions that indicate students want to move forward, do more math, or try something harder. These are music to our ears! "What's the next question?" "We want to try a harder problem, is that okay?" "When you say numbers that add to 10, do we only get to use whole numbers?"

When your students ask proximity questions and stop-thinking questions, Liljedahl (2021, pp. 89–90) suggests responding with a question that puts the thinking back on them (see Figure 3.4).

Figure 3.4 · *Questions That Elicit Student Thinking*

> ➢ Isn't that interesting?
> ➢ Can you find something else?
> ➢ Can you show me how you did that?
> ➢ Is that always true?
> ➢ Why do you think that is?
> ➢ Are you sure? Does that make sense?
> ➢ Why don't you try something else?
> ➢ Why don't you try another one?
> ➢ Are you asking me or telling me?

HOW DO I SELECT JUST-RIGHT MATH ROUTINES?

In addition to selecting or creating just-right tasks, you might also consider some of the rich math routines that are now at our fingertips as tasks. A math routine is both structured and adaptable; it is a structure that facilitates student thinking and is adaptable enough to be used over and over while maintaining high levels of rigor with each repeated use. Some routines, such as "Which One Doesn't Belong?," can serve as terrific focus activities during your warm-up or launch. Other routines, such as "Notice and Wonder," lend themselves to increased communication. There are so many great routines available to us that you could use a different one every day and still not exhaust the list.

> A math routine is both structured and adaptable; it is a structure that facilitates student thinking and is adaptable enough to be used over and over while maintaining high levels of rigor with each repeated use.

That said, note that the power of a routine reveals itself when it is used routinely, not just once or twice. You will want to take time to explicitly teach the routines to students to maximize the benefit. Therefore, you might find it helpful to teach routines during whole-class instruction and then lean into those same routines during your small group sessions.

In Figure 3.5, you will find a list of a few amazing routines that you may consider using with your teacher-facilitated small groups.

Check out the links for the math routines listed by visiting the companion website at resources.corwin.com/ mathsmallgroups.

Figure 3.5 • *Math Routines Worth Checking Out*

Routine	Description
Bet-Line	Word problem routine based on predicting what comes next
Esti-Mysteries	Number sense routine that uses riddles to find the total
Math Flips	Number sense routine with visual cues for students
Math Talks	Number and operations routines based on mental math strategies
Notice and Wonder	Thinking routine based on what students notice and wonder

Routine	Description
Rough Draft Thinking	Communication routine where students share their thinking throughout the problem-solving process
Splat!	Number sense routine with visual cues for students
Target the Question	Word problem routine that poses different questions using the same prompt
Think Pair Share	Thinking routine where students think independently, talk in pairs, then share with the group
Three Reads Protocol	Word problem routine where students relate to the story, identify quantities and relationships, and predict the math question
Which One Doesn't Belong?	Thinking routine where students identify similarities and differences between and among four numbers, quantities, shapes, etc.

HOW DO I PLAN WHAT TO DO BEFORE, DURING, AND AFTER THE TASK?

If you're asking this question, look again at the "How do I avoid show-and-tell teaching?" section previously discussed. In simple terms, you want to launch the task as quickly as possible without giving away the thinking. This may be accomplished with a quick stand-up meeting, followed by students being seated to explore the idea further.

During the Explore phase, ask prompting and probing questions and offer prompts only as needed. Avoid the temptation to jump in too soon, and never take a student's writing tool from them for the purpose of showing them how to do the math. You do not want to steal the thinking from your students!

And finally, after students have had sufficient exploration time, debrief the task by asking prompting and probing questions, addressing misconceptions, and reviewing or preteaching vocabulary, and provide just enough input to ensure all students have advanced in their understanding.

CAN I USE GAMES DURING MY MATH SMALL GROUP SESSIONS?

Of course! Games can make great warm-up and practice/application activities, as well as explorations. Keep in mind that not all games are created equal. Some games provide great opportunities for pushing your students' thinking forward. Others provide nothing more than worksheet-like practice using cards or dice, which, while fun, are not likely to advance students' understanding of the concept or topic. So, select your games carefully!

Here are some questions to consider as you evaluate whether a game is right for your students:

- Does it align with your mathematical learning target?
- Is it at the correct level of rigor for your learning target and student needs?
- Does it have an element of chance or strategy that makes it fun for students to play again and again?
- Does it encourage a strategy?

AT THE END OF THE LESSON, HOW DO I HELP MY STUDENTS SEE THAT LEARNING TOOK PLACE?

During the last part of the lesson, whether you consider it a synthesis or a discuss/debrief, be sure to collect evidence of student learning for a variety of reasons—to celebrate learning success, determine next steps, or restructure group membership, among others. There are many ways you might achieve this goal, and here are a few:

▸ **Connections and Reflections:** Ask prompting and probing questions that lead students to make connections and then reflect on their learning. You may use a checklist or record annotations to collect evidence of student learning during the discussion.

▸ **Ticket Out the Door:** Give students one problem to solve to use as a check for understanding. Often, these exit tickets help you determine what to address in the small group on the next day.

▸ **Academic Vocabulary:** Many students struggle with math vocabulary because it is not commonly used outside of math class. During your closure, you might take a moment to review or to preteach vocabulary. A quick and simple way to do this is to have the words written on wooden sticks. Pull out one at a time, and ask students to draw a sketch or show a predetermined hand signal to represent that word.

▸ **Anchor Charts:** Whenever possible, refer back to anchor charts used during whole group math instruction. It is important to connect small group learning to what is discussed as a whole class.

▸ **Journal Prompts:** Consider using a two-part journal prompt such as
  o What I now understand about _____ is . . .
  o A picture of that is . . .

  Additional journal prompts might include the following:
  o I'm most excited that . . .
  o The hardest part was . . .
  o I helped someone else when . . .
  o I needed help with . . .
  o I'm still wondering about . . .

HOW DO I MAKE SURE I DON'T FORGET ANYTHING?

You may want to consider creating a checklist to help you systematize your preparation. The sample pictured in Figure 3.6 may help you get started.

> You may want to consider creating a checklist to help you systematize your preparation. The sample pictured in Figure 3.6 may help you get started.

Figure 3.6 · *Sample Preparation Checklist*

Teacher-Facilitated Math Small Group Preparation Checklist

This list provides a summary of the steps to take in preparation for teacher-facilitated math small groups.

✓	Task	Notes
	Determine Targeted Math Content and Small Group Members	
	Unwrap grade-level standard(s) for current grade-level unit	
	Use *Math Small Group* Standards Trajectory Document to identify possible unfinished learning from previous grades	
	Create learning targets for teacher-facilitated math small group	
	Determine direct connections between the teacher-facilitated math small group learning targets and the current grade-level math content	
	Collect whole group data to determine which students might need support with unfinished learning	
	Prepare structure and activities for other students ▸ Centers/workstations ▸ Task cards ▸ Independent work ▸ Group work ▸ Asynchronous self-selected activities	

(Continued)

Figure 3.6 · (Continued)

✓	Task	Notes
	Prepare for Teacher-Facilitated Math Small Groups	
	Plan using the Eb4E Lesson Planning Template ▸ Select/create task ▸ Anticipate student responses ▸ Prepare prompting and probing questions	
	Prepare data collection student record (2 options)	
	Collect math tools and place in Mathematicians Tool Kit	
	Collect teacher materials	
	Select and prepare work space and work stance (stand up or sit down)	

[online resources] **To download this template, visit resources.corwin.com/mathsmallgroups.**

YOUR TURN

This chapter focused on specific issues you will want to consider as you plan for your teacher-facilitated math small groups. The ways in which you engage your students, keep them on track, and keep their learning front and center really matter! Take a few minutes now to reflect on what you just read and how you will integrate it into your math small group plan.

Learning Intention

After reading this chapter, you will have a better idea of how to plan for your math small group lessons.

Success Criteria

You will be able to plan for all components of your math small group lessons using one of the sample math small group lesson plan sequences or a sequence of your choice.

- What new ideas or good reminders did you glean from this chapter?
- Using one of the planning templates linked on this page or another of your choice, sketch out a sample math small group lesson you might use with your students. There are two templates to choose from: the LED planner (Learn-Explore-Debrief/Discuss) and the WCPS planner (Warm-Up, Concept Development, Practice and Application, and Synthesis).

To download the Eb4E Lesson Planning Template, visit resources.corwin.com/mathsmallgroups.

CHAPTER 4

TARGETING THE MATH, SUPPORTING THE STUDENTS, PROVIDING ACCESS FOR ALL

Learning Intention

After reading this chapter, you will understand the purpose of targeting the math. This includes identifying strengths and learning pathways when preparing for your teacher-facilitated math small groups.

Success Criteria

You will be able to identify the three steps for planning that comprise the Math Small Group Framework and describe how you will use this framework to support your work with math small groups.

CHAPTER INTRODUCTION

Chapters 1–3 provided you with the background and practical advice for getting your teacher-facilitated math small groups planned and prepared. We've been gradually addressing these three questions first introduced in Chapter 1:

1) How do I set up math small groups?
2) What do I do with the students once they're in the small group?
3) What do I do with the rest of the students while I'm working with small groups?

Questions 1 and 3 were addressed in the first two chapters, and question 2 was partially addressed in Chapter 3. As we shift into Chapter 4, we are going to address what is perhaps the biggest piece of the puzzle: How do you select the just-right math content to address in your math small groups? How do you lean into your grade-level content while attending to prerequisite concepts and skills that may need additional attention? This chapter serves not only as the final step in preparing to teach math small groups, but also as a transition to Part B, where you will have multiple options from which you can select the just-right math trajectory for the content you wish to address.

LET THE MATH TAKE THE LEAD

Now that we've talked about the logistics and preparation for building your teacher-facilitated math small groups, it's time to talk about the mathematics you are addressing. As you have likely experienced firsthand, students walk through our classroom doors every day with such varied experiences and vast differences in their mathematical backgrounds and understandings. No two students have the same mathematical profile, making the flexibility mentioned in previous chapters even more necessary.

So . . . it's really the math that must take the lead when it comes to making decisions about your math small group instruction. Your grade-level content guides you in what topics to address and what rigor levels to target. Based on student readiness, the content in previous grade levels may need to be nested in the grade-level work you do. And for those students ready for more, you need to know how deep your grade-level content goes and when it's time to move ahead into future content. The knowledge of how to do this is at the heart of small group math instruction.

Before we dive into the strategies for making this possible, it's important to know the role collegiality plays in this effort (Karp et al., 2021). After all, we're talking about math trajectories that begin before your students cross your threshold and end long after they move on. This makes collaboration with your colleagues all the more important. Meeting with them to discuss common practices and understanding regarding mathematics will make your job easier and your students' experiences richer.

What I'm talking about here is creating a math whole-school agreement, as discussed in *The Math Pact, Elementary* (Karp et al., 2021). Your work will be enriched when you and your colleagues agree and adhere to using certain vocabulary, notations, symbols, procedures, rules, generalizations, and the like. Not doing so completely undermines the goals of your effort in designing excellent whole-class and small group instruction. Meeting within and across grade levels to reach these agreements enhances the entire math learning journey for each and every student in your school.

If you would like to design a mathematics whole-school agreement with your colleagues, you will want to work with your site leaders to put together a system that meshes with your current meeting schedule. Perhaps doing this work during grade-level meetings, vertical articulation sessions, or whole-staff workshops might work. Basically, you will want to choose a topic that needs coherence within and across grade levels (see Figure 4.1 for a short list of possible topic categories). Each grade level discusses just one topic, coming to agreement for how to address that particular issue, whether it be a problem-solving protocol, proper vocabulary, instructional strategy, or the like. Then multiple grade levels come together to reach consensus regarding that topic. The more topics you handle this way, the greater the mathematical coherence you will achieve.

> To learn more about creating a Math Whole-School Agreement, check out *The Math Pact* series (2021) and "13 Rules That Expire" (2014) by by Karen S. Karp, Barbara J. Dougherty, and Sarah B. Bush.

Figure 4.1 • *Topics to Discuss Within and Across Grade Levels*

❖ Using Correct and Consistent Mathematical Language
❖ Noting the Importance of Precise Notation
❖ Using Cohesive and Consistent Representations
❖ Evaluating Rules That Expire*
❖ Developing Common Instructional Strategies
❖ Eliminating Teaching by Telling

*Check out their article "13 Rules That Expire" (Karp et al., 2014), published by NCTM.

THE MATH SMALL GROUP FRAMEWORK

Letting the math take the lead is another way to say that we will target the math when it comes to math small groups. The point is that we are targeting the math rather than the students. We deconstruct the standards, study the trajectories, identify pathways and connections, and collect formative data. Then we analyze the strengths of our students, looking at what they *do* know, how they learn best, how they represent their thinking, and how they express their learning. Only then do we enter the planning phase, where we connect the math content with group membership processes. This helps ensure that students are working in optimal settings for every math concept, not simply targeted to be in the low, medium, or high math group for the year.

The Math Small Group Framework (Figure 4.2) provides a three-step approach to small group instruction. It begins with a focus on the math, shifts into identifying teacher and student strengths, and then finally moves into the design phase by creating pathways for students to engage in math small group instruction.

Figure 4.2 • *Teacher-Facilitated Math Small Group Framework*

STEP 1 **Focus on Math**	• Deconstruct grade-level standard(s) of focus • Study the corresponding K-6 standards trajectory • Identify pathway concepts/skills that connect to grade-level standards • Collect formative data based on the learning pathway

STEP 2
Identify Strengths
	• Identify teacher strengths
	• Identify learner strengths
	  ○ What's the last thing students understand along the learning pathway?
	  ○ How do they engage with, represent, and express their learning?

STEP 3 **Create Pathways**	• Use the Explore Before Explain (Eb4E) approach • Ascertain what students *do* know • Connect small group work and whole-class learning in both settings

Step 1: Focus on Math

During Step 1, the Focus on Math phase, you target the mathematics you want to focus on. At this step, you primarily dive into grade-level expectations for all students, unwrap current grade-level standards, and study the standards that come before and after. During this process, you identify math learning targets for whole group instruction as well as for your teacher-facilitated math small groups. Then you collect and analyze formative assessment data to inform you about instruction and your students about their learning.

> As an aside, formative assessment data should always be shared with students as a way to help them know where they are and set goals for where to go next (Liljedahl, 2021).

NOT LONG AGO, Tara was preparing to begin her fractions unit. As she dove into the content, she knew there were some areas where she would need to support her students as they grappled with new ideas. That said, she also knew the importance of targeting the math rather than the students. She spent time deconstructing her fractions standards so she knew clearly what she would be addressing in the coming weeks. She anticipated ways in which her students might display misconceptions. She looked at ways in which she might need to bridge content from previous grade levels and how those fractions ideas could be quickly connected to her on-grade-level standards.

Most importantly, *she kept her focus on the math*. She needed to wait until the students had a chance to show her what they already knew and understood before deciding what supports each would need. Not until she had those data would she be able to determine group membership and next steps. For the time being, she simply targeted the math, knowing she would learn more about the students after they got the chance to show her. ●

Deconstruct Grade-Level Standards of Focus

Prior to planning your math small group instruction, take some time to dive deeply into the mathematics standards you'll be addressing. The standards themselves reveal the rigor level, content parameters, vocabulary, and representations important for success. This is also a good time to reflect on your math whole school agreement, if your school has one in place, to ensure you use the agreed-upon strategies, rules, vocabulary, symbols, and so on.

Begin by closely examining the standard(s) for your upcoming math unit of study. It is important to understand not only the standard you are targeting, but how that standard relates to others both within the grade and in the grades before and after yours. The *Math Small Group* Standards Trajectory Document offers a map that shows how all the standards for each domain interrelate. Similarly, you can also use Achieve the Core's Coherence Map to guide your thinking. As you analyze the standards, here are the questions to ask yourself:

▸ To be successful with the on-grade-level content in this standard, what should students know and be able to do?

▸ What should the learning targets state?

▸ How will I get my students from where they currently are to this new place on their learning pathway?

> The *Math Small Group* Standards Trajectory Document offers a map that shows how all the standards for each domain interrelate. To download this tool, visit resources. corwin.com/mathsmallgroups.

> To find Achieve the Core's Coherence Map, visit https:// achievethecore.org/page/1118/coherence-map.

As you examine the trajectories, consider using planning tools to guide your thinking about how to connect the standards to your lessons. The Deconstructing Standards Planning Template (Figure 4.3) provides a way for you to dive deep into the standard(s) and attend to the depth and breadth of the standard(s). The Standards Trajectory Document Planning Template (Figure 4.4) provides a structure for you to consider as you connect standards within and across grade levels to the lesson plans you will create for your math small groups.

Figure 4.3 · *Deconstructing Standards Planning Template*

Using the *Math Small Group* Standards Trajectory Document, focus on your grade-level standard to determine what students should know and be able to do. Then focus on the corresponding standards in previous grade levels to determine the skills/concepts where students may have unfinished learning. How will you purposefully connect the unfinished learning to grade-level expectations in *every* math small group session?

Grade-Level Standard(s) for Current Unit of Study: Copy and paste standard(s) here. Highlight verbs in green, nouns/noun phrases in red, and adverbial phrases in yellow.		
What should students know? (nouns)	**What should students be able to do?** (verbs)	**What are the parameters?** (adverbial phrases)
What unfinished learning may exist from previous grade-level standards?	**How will you connect the unfinished learning to current grade-level math goals during your teacher-facilitated math small group?**	
Possible Daily Learning Targets	**Possible Learning Experiences (tasks, questions, connections)**	**Evidence of Student Learning**

online resources **To download this template, visit resources.corwin.com/mathsmallgroups.**

Figure 4.4 • *Standards Trajectory Document Planning Template*

Math Small Group **Standards Trajectory Document Planning Template**

Download the *Math Small Group* Standards Trajectory Document on the companion website.

Select one math concept on which to focus in this template. What do you notice as you read the standards across the grade levels? Highlight the standard for your targeted grade level. How do the standards in the previous grade level(s) support it? How do the standards in later grade level(s) extend it? What math concepts or skills from previous grade levels may need to be targeted to help students gain access to the grade-level content? How does this inform your planning for your math small groups?

Selected Grade-Level Standard (copy and paste into the space below)	What do you notice/ wonder as you read the corresponding standards for the grade levels before and after?	What math concepts or skills from previous grade levels may need to be targeted to help students gain access to the grade-level content?

online resources **To download this template, visit resources.corwin.com/mathsmallgroups.**

Study the Corresponding K–5 Math Content Trajectory

Part B in this book lays out the Math Content Trajectories for most of the major math domains taught in Grades K–5. Each of these trajectories corresponds to the much more detailed standards trajectories found in the *Math Small Group Standards Trajectory Document*. Take time to study the appropriate trajectory, looking at the math that was addressed prior to, within, and after your grade level. The more familiar you become with the below- and above-level standards, the easier you will find it to spontaneously dip down (or up) while connecting to your on-grade-level standards during your math small group sessions.

As you focus on the standards in the grades before and after yours, ask yourself the following questions. You may find it helpful to download the Math Content Trajectory Reflection (see Figure 4.5) and use it to guide your thinking as you contemplate the K–5 Math Content Trajectories.

> You may find it helpful to download the Math Content Trajectory Reflection from the companion website and use it to guide your thinking as you contemplate the K–5 Math Content Trajectories.

Identify Pathway Concepts/Skills That Connect to Grade-Level Standards

When planning for your math small groups, consider the pathway within and across grade levels that will benefit your students. Many students exhibit unfinished previous learning at one time or another, and the more you know about the math content pathways, the better prepared you will be to temporarily work with out-of-grade-level standards as you accelerate students through the prerequisite work and back to their grade-level expectations.

Finally, identify the concepts/skills from the previous grade's standards where you think unfinished learning might appear in your class. Use that information to anticipate needed learning targets, create observation forms, and design formative assessment tasks to detect any unfinished learning that might exist.

Collect Formative Data

Based on the information gleaned from examining the standards and the math content trajectories, create formative assessments that will help you determine group membership for your math small groups. Remember that formative assessment can take many forms. (See Chapter 3 for multiple suggestions.)

Figure 4.5 · *Math Content Trajectory Reflection Questions*

Using the *Math Small Group* Standards Trajectory Document, focus on your grade-level standard to determine what students should know and be able to do. Then focus on the corresponding standards in previous grade levels to determine the skills/concepts where students may have unfinished learning. Also consider the above-grade-level standards to extend the thinking in your math small groups. How will you purposefully connect the out-of-grade-level learning to grade-level expectations in *every* math small group session?

Based on your current content, what is most important for students to understand?
What prerequisite understandings related to your current content do you see in the previous grade levels?
How might you support your students with prior-grade-level content in a connected way?
How will you avoid the temptation to reteach entire units of study?
How might you connect the prior-grade-level content to your on-grade-level content every time you meet with your math small groups?
What content that appears on the trajectory is typically covered after your grade level?
What curiosities about future content might you address in your math small groups?

online resources ⌂ **To download this template, visit resources.corwin.com/mathsmallgroups.**

Step 2: Identify Strengths

In Step 2, the Identify Strengths phase, you identify both your strengths and those of your students, concentrating on what they *do* know and do as well as how they engage with, represent, and express their learning.

Identify Teacher Strengths

In the Math Small Group Framework, I suggest that you identify your strengths in this area as well. This means both your content knowledge and your pedagogical expertise. Do you own the specialized content knowledge necessary for teaching the content? Do you know the specific related instructional strategies and multiple representations for helping students develop full understanding? How might you use your expertise and strengths to guide your students in their learning?

> If you find that you need additional content or pedagogical expertise, you may want to engage in standards study using the *Math Small Group* Standards Trajectory Document. To download, visit resources.corwin.com/mathsmallgroups.

> A great resource for studying math content and pedagogy is the *Teaching Student-Centered Mathematics* books by John Van de Walle, LouAnn Lovin, Karen Karp, and Jennifer Bay-Williams. They are available for Grades K–3, 3–5, and 5–8.

Identify Learner Strengths

For many years, we have focused our efforts on differentiation and intervention. These structures have contributed to helping us understand how to move students forward in their mathematical understanding. When done well, these foundational elements of instruction support learners as they fill identified learning gaps, and they also give us the chance to build, massage, and evolve our theories.

More recently, we have come to understand that, when translated into practice, these structures often fall short, as they tend to focus more on what the child is missing rather than on the assets that abound inside each child (Chardin & Novak, 2021; Kobett & Karp, 2020). For example, differentiation tends to be responsive, focused on individual disability, and based on cause and effect. In contrast, Universal Design for Learning tends to be proactive, focused on variability among students, and intentional (CAST, 2018). By focusing on students' strengths and being intentional in our planning, we tap into ways we can best support our students. We honor the learning that has already taken place and can build upon and connect to what has come before.

MELISSA WAS WORKING on developing number sense with her young students, focusing on composing and decomposing numbers within 10. Because she wanted each student to function within their strengths, she designed her math small groups to offer as much choice as possible. Her students were already familiar with ten frames, rekenereks, and number bonds, so she put out two baskets that had enough supplies for each student to select their representation of choice. Not only did she offer them a choice of math tools, but she also provided them with whiteboards and markers as well as paper and pencil so they could record their thinking in ways that suited them. And finally, when she asked prompting and probing questions, she offered temporary supports for students as needed, giving them opportunities to verbalize their thinking in ways that allowed their strengths to shine. ●

Step 3: Create Pathways

In Step 3, the Create Pathways phase, you create pathways and scaffolds for students to access grade-level content. This is where all the preparation you learned about in Chapters 1–3 comes into play.

Use the Eb4E Approach

For example, you may want to consider the Explore Before Explain (Eb4E) approach as it serves as a great format for any setting, including the small group setting. This approach establishes that the best learning takes place when students engage in tasks *without* being shown what to do first. When using this protocol, you launch the session by briefly introducing the task; provide students with time to explore and grapple with that task; and then facilitate a discussion about what students notice, wonder, and learned. It's only in this Discuss phase that you might explicitly provide input to students as needed. Note that either of the sample lesson planning structures shared in Chapter 3 can be used to support the Eb4E approach, provided you avoid show-and-tell teaching. In an effort to emphasize this, the Launch-Explore-Discuss structure is used in the sample activities found in Chapters 5–12.

Ascertain What Students *Do* Know

As previously mentioned, there are many data sources that you might draw from to learn more about your students' current mathematical understandings. Of course, you can certainly use information gleaned from larger assessments such as benchmark or diagnostic tests. However, the most current data, preferably from formative assessments, will be most useful in determining what students know at this point in time. These might include weekly common formative assessments, daily cool-down or exit tickets, completed classroom tasks, or observational notes.

When analyzing multiple forms of data, take care to focus on the assets students bring to the table, not their deficits. Home in on what they did well, not where they offered incorrect solutions. Pay attention to their communication, representations, and organizational style.

If possible, use multiple data sets so you can triangulate your data rather than using one source in order to capture a full picture of each student instead of one simple isolated idea. Create an assets-based math profile for each student, such as the one shown in Figure 4.6. In doing so, you will create your math small groups more wisely as well as plan more interesting, varied, and challenging tasks for them. Don't they deserve that?

Figure 4.6 · *Sample Assets-Based Math Profile*

Prompts adapted from *Strengths-Based Teaching and Learning in Mathematics* (2020) by Kobett and Karp.

Math Concept: _____ Student: _____ Date: _____

Based on various data sources, rank student on a scale of 1–6 for each prompt below. Cite evidence for why you chose that ranking.

Mathematical Practices

Category	Rank 1–6	Evidence
Mathematical Rigor Conceptual Understanding ▸ Asks and answers "why" questions ▸ Focuses on sensemaking ▸ Uses physical objects, visuals, and explanations to make thinking visible Procedural Fluency ▸ Solves problems accurately ▸ Solves problems efficiently ▸ Solves problems flexibly ▸ Solves problems appropriately Application ▸ Decontextualizes quantities, relationships, and operations ▸ Contextualizes mathematical problems		

Category	Rank 1–6	Evidence
Productive Disposition Sees math as sensible, useful, and worthwhile Perseveres through struggle Exhibits confidence in math ability		

Communication
Oral Explanation
  ▸ Organizes explanations
  ▸ Explains reasoning
  ▸ Explains different strategies
  ▸ Uses precise vocabulary
Listening
  ▸ Listens to others speak
  ▸ Does not interrupt
  ▸ Asks strategic follow-up questions that connect to the strategy or solution		

Representations Uses tools strategically Explains why tools were selected Models the math correctly		
Connections Connects physical, visual, symbolic, verbal, and contextual representations Looks for and makes use of structure Looks for and expresses regularity in repeated reasoning		

online resources ▸ **To download this template, visit resources.corwin.com/mathsmallgroups.**

Connect Small Group and Whole-Class Learning in Both Settings

One last step to keep in mind when planning for your math small groups is to be mindful of ways you connect math learning across settings. Whenever possible, use the same manipulatives and visuals, the same anchor charts, and the same vocabulary to help students connect their learning across experiences. Several ideas for making these connections were addressed in Chapter 2. Deliberate action in this way will make your job easier and help students transfer and apply their learning with more frequency and accuracy.

YOUR TURN

In this chapter, you read about ways in which you might target the specific mathematics concepts to work on in order to support students where they are. Identifying students' strengths plays a critical role in ensuring students connect new learning to what they already know as well as to on-grade-level expectations. As you contemplate how you will embed these ideas into your work, take a few minutes to reflect on the following questions.

Learning Intention

After reading this chapter, you will understand the purpose of targeting the math. This includes identifying strengths and learning pathways when preparing for your teacher-facilitated math small groups.

Success Criteria

You will be able to identify the three steps of planning that comprise the Math Small Group Framework and describe how you will use this framework to support your work with math small groups.

- Can you describe the three steps of the Math Small Group Framework and explain why each is important?
- How will you use each of these three steps to support your planning and implementation of your teacher-facilitated math small groups?
- How will you go about targeting the math and supporting all students?

PART B

PLANNING FOR AND TEACHING MATH SMALL GROUPS

HOW TO USE PART B

This section will provide you with examples for designing small group math lessons based on your targeted math concept(s). It includes sample trajectories and activities to model what learning pathways might look like for your teacher-facilitated math small groups, always connecting to your current grade-level content.

Each chapter includes a math content trajectory that focuses on a major chunk of K–5 mathematics and how it evolves across the grade levels over time. Each trajectory and activity provides you with a sampling of how you might simply create a math small group session using the Eb4E approach. Because every situation will be different, there are simple reminders to connect back to the specific grade-level content on which you're working. That piece is critical for success.

For example, when working on fifth-grade fraction multiplication, your formative assessment data may reveal that a few of your students would benefit from revisiting array-based whole-number multiplication. To find a sample lesson, go to Chapter 9, which focuses on multiplication and division, to view supports you may find helpful: materials, representations, trajectories, strengths-finder tips, and the like. Then you can view the sample activity to get an idea for how to set up a small group experience.

Each activity is comprised of Launch, Explore, and Discuss prompts as well as a reminder to complete checks for understanding and a connection back to grade-level content.

The features in this section are as follows:

- **Math Tools:** This section lets you know the general materials needed to work with the content. Since you will occasionally be connecting current content with out-of-grade-level content during your math small groups, these lists are intended to speed up your preparation by telling you up front which tools will be most useful.

- **Math Content Trajectories:** This section provides you with a broad overview of the standards that typically fall within the continuum. Following each trajectory, you'll find a description titled About This Trajectory. Since the content you're looking to work on with a teacher-facilitated small group may exist outside the grade level you currently teach, this information provides you with some background content to help you prepare for your targeted math small groups.

- **Algebraic Thinking and Overarching Structures:** Algebraic thinking content such as word problem types, and structures such as properties of operations, are often taught initially as isolated concepts. Then they are frequently revisited while studying other math topics. This feature provides ideas for how you might embed concepts classified as algebraic thinking within and across math concepts.

- **Prompts for Determining Learners' Strengths:** These sample questions are intended to help you pinpoint the last thing your students know along the trajectory so you know just where to start. They also help your students focus on the math content being targeted.

- **Sample Lessons:** Using the Explore Before Explain (Eb4E) approach, each sample lesson follows the Launch-Explore-Discuss cycle. You can just as easily use the Warm-Up-Concept Development-Application-Cool Down approach for each activity if you prefer. Keep in mind that throughout the lesson, making explicit connections to on-level content will focus the students on their current grade-level standards.

CHAPTER 5

COUNTING AND CARDINALITY

Learning Intention

After reading this chapter, you will understand how to target the math, identify strengths, and plan pathways for content related to Counting and Cardinality.

Success Criteria

You will be able to use the math content trajectory for Counting and Cardinality, in addition to your State Standards Framework or the *Math Small Group* Standards Trajectory Document, to help you identify the just-right starting place for your students.

CHAPTER INTRODUCTION

Counting and Cardinality concepts are addressed directly in early grades, usually in kindergarten. During those early years, students gain proficiency in connecting the counting sequence with counting objects and numeral recognition. Numeral writing is often incorporated into this domain as well.

Although this domain is typically considered complete by the end of kindergarten, you may want to consider the implications of these skills with increasingly larger number sets. As they progress through the grade levels, students work with numbers within 100 in Grade 1, within 1,000 in Grades 2–3, and within 1,000,000+ in Grades 4–5. In addition, students work directly with numbers that have digits to the right of the decimal point in Grades 4–5. Although the counting, numeral recognition, and numeral writing activities at higher levels tend to be included with place value standards, they could be considered extensions of the Counting and Cardinality domain as well. You may want to consider using the activities in this chapter for larger number sets, as all students in Grades K–5 would benefit from thinking about the counting sequence and pattern of the count in similar ways as we teach in kindergarten.

COUNTING AND CARDINALITY: AN OVERVIEW

The counting sequence seems so simple to us, but for young children, it can be quite a feat to learn to count to 10, then to 20, and then to 100. Most children learn the counting sequence first, at least in chunks, learning the verbal patterns prior to using the sequence to count objects. It's important to note that the most difficult decade in the counting sequence is found near the beginning: 11 through 19. Known as the "teen" numbers, the number names in this passage do not follow the verbal pattern, with the words *eleven* and *twelve* not following any kind of pattern. Many students successfully count from 20 to 100 prior to solidly counting from 11 to 19.

Next, students apply the counting sequence to counting sets of objects, coordinating with one-to-one correspondence. Eventually, you can tell if they've achieved cardinality when they correctly answer the question "How many did you count?" by indicating that the last counting number they said indicates the total number of objects in the set.

Finally, students learn to coordinate their understanding of the quantity, the number name, and the numeral that matches. Note that numeral writing often becomes an issue, as students need to not only identify the numeral that matches the number name but also write it. Learning to write numerals can be compared to learning to write letters—it's a pre-math skill and yet critically important in becoming math literate (or numerate). You'll want to provide students with ample opportunities to practice writing their numerals in ways that help them connect the written numeral to their respective quantities.

The last item in this trajectory is skip counting. Not only should students playfully count by tens, fives, twos, and so on, but they should also have the opportunity to conceptually skip count with objects, seeing the connection between the numbers and the quantities.

In Chapter 4, we discussed the Math Small Group Framework. The content in the rest of this chapter will follow the structure of the framework, pictured again in Figure 5.1.

Figure 5.1 • *Teacher-Facilitated Math Small Group Framework*

STEP 1 **Focus on Math**	• Deconstruct grade-level standard(s) of focus • Study the corresponding K-6 standards trajectory • Identify pathway concepts/skills that connect to grade-level standards • Collect formative data based on the learning pathway

STEP 2
Identify Strengths
	• Identify teacher strengths
	• Identify learner strengths
	  ○ What's the last thing students understand along the learning pathway?
	  ○ How do they engage with, represent, and express their learning?

STEP 3 **Create Pathways**	• Use the Explore Before Explain (Eb4E) approach • Ascertain what students *do* know • Connect small group work and whole-class learning in both settings

FOCUS ON MATH: MATH CONTENT TRAJECTORY FOR COUNTING AND CARDINALITY

The first step in the framework is to Focus on Math. Here, you will want to go through four processes to ensure you identify the necessary content for your students. Although Counting and Cardinality is primarily an early childhood domain, be sure to account for counting and numeral writing throughout the grade levels, including numerals with digits on both sides of the decimal point. When working with larger numbers, there will be a significant overlap with the place value standards.

The four processes to engage in as you Focus on Math are as follows:

1. Identify and deconstruct the grade-level standard(s) relevant to Counting and Cardinality.

2. Study the Counting and Cardinality standards trajectory in this chapter (see Figure 5.2) as well as in the *Math Small Group* Standards Trajectory Document.

3. Identify the multigrade-level pathway concepts and skills that connect to on-grade-level standards for Counting and Cardinality. This may include standards from previous grade levels as well as standards for future grade levels. Use whichever standards you need based on the structure (heterogeneous, Guided Math, etc.) and goals for your math small groups.

4. Collect formative data based on the Counting and Cardinality standards. Your formative data may include daily entrance or exit tickets, weekly common formative assessments, classroom observational data, or any other data you collect on a regular basis.

Figure 5.2 · *Trajectory for Counting and Cardinality*

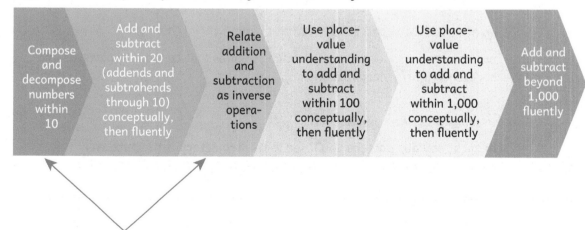

The *Math Small Group* Standards Trajectory Document provides a detailed view of the learning trajectory by showing how standards progress across the grade levels. To download this tool, visit resources.corwin.com/mathsmallgroups.

With the Counting and Cardinality trajectory, keep in mind that counting verbally and counting objects overlap considerably. Although they appear to be sequential in Figure 5.2, children learn the counting sequence while learning to count objects using one-to-one correspondence.

The explicit topics included in the Counting and Cardinality trajectory typically appear in kindergarten for most state standards. That said, several elements in this trajectory repeat with different number sets. For example, for many State Standards Frameworks,

- kindergarten students typically count verbally to 100 from any number and count objects and write numerals through 20;
- first graders count verbally, represent quantities, and write numerals through 120;
- second and third graders count verbally, represent quantities, and write numerals within 1,000; and
- fourth graders count verbally, represent quantities, and write numerals within 1,000,000.

Of course, when representing numbers within 100, 1,000, and 1,000,000, students are also typically asked to think about place value principles as well. Those activities can be found in Chapter 7 of this book.

This trajectory provides you with a visual for how the content progresses. You will want to reference your state standards documents or the *Math Small Group* Standards Trajectory Document for a more detailed look at how these standards progress over time.

Algebraic Thinking and Overarching Structures

This trajectory includes two overarching themes that connect to patterns and representations/generalizations.

Patterns and Generalizations

The most obvious pattern you'll see in this trajectory is the pattern of the count. Students should have opportunities to hear the patterns as they engage in rote counting as well as when they are counting. Furthermore, you can also prompt them to discover patterns in the written count, whether counting by ones or counting by other amounts. Be sure your students experience the vertical number line (see Object 5.1), where they can see that 0–9 repeats over and over in the ones place while, in the tens place, they can see ten 1s, followed by ten 2s, followed by ten 3s, and so on. Ask your students why that is and why it's important.

Object 5.1 · *The Pattern of the Count on a Vertical Number Line*

30
29
28
27
26
25
24
23
22
21
20
19
18
17
16
15
14
13
12
11
10
9
8
7
6
5
4
3
2
1
0

Strategies and Representations

The representations that most frequently appear in the standards include those items that will help your students connect quantities, number names, and numerals. These typically include tools like counters for working on numbers within 20 and base-ten manipulatives for working on numbers within 100, 1,000, or higher. Your students can arrange manipulatives such as ten frames and rekenreks as well as visuals such as number tracks in different ways and match them to written numerals (see Objects 5.2 and 5.3).

Object 5.2 • *Arrangements for 13 Using Multicolor Counters*

Object 5.3 • *Arrangements for 254 Using KP® Ten-Frame Tiles and Base-Ten Blocks*

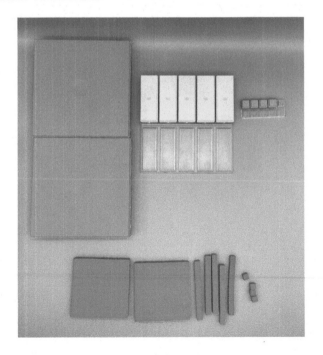

Learn more about KP® Ten-Frame Tiles at
www.kpmathematics.com.

MATH TOOLS TO SUPPORT THIS TRAJECTORY

When preparing for your teacher-facilitated math small groups, you
may be planning for math concepts and skills that are not necessarily at your
grade level. The suggestions in this section are intended to help you think
through the materials you may need, especially for facilitating conceptual
development. As mentioned in Chapter 3, having your materials at your
fingertips will protect your small group time from interruptions to collect
needed materials.

As you gather materials, be mindful that you include a wide variety so as to
encourage students to translate within and across the different categories
of representations: concrete (manipulatives and objects), visual, symbolic,
verbal, and contextual (Lesh et al., 1987). You should encourage students to
represent their thinking in ways that make sense to them, giving them choice as
much as possible. In addition, ask students to work side by side with different
representations and then compare and contrast what they see. This will help
students make sense of their thinking as well as develop new ways of thinking
about the concepts and skills at hand.

See Chapter 2 for more information about the Lesh
Translation Model of Representations.

Concrete Representations

Counters: Any small, countable objects will suffice such as round color counters,
unit squares, small erasers, cereal bits, beans, and the like. In addition, placing
objects and ten frames and using rekenereks allow students to touch the objects
as they count them.

Linking Cubes: Cubes that link together may be used as number tracks. Although
number lines are a common visual used across grade levels, young children
frequently confuse the tick marks rather than the number of "jumps," or spaces
between the tick marks, as indicating the quantity. Instead, number tracks
may be created using linking cubes, with the number of cubes representing the
quantity (see Object 5.4).

Object 5.4 · *Number Tracks Using Linking Cubes*

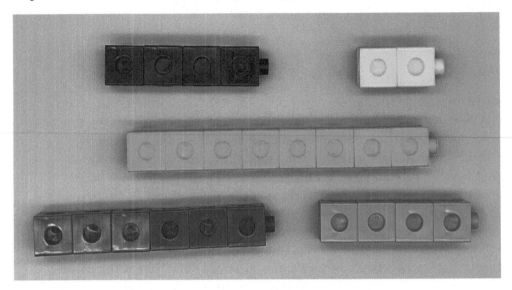

Visual Representations

Number and Numeral Cards: You can use numeral and number cards for students to gain fluency with numeral recognition and matching numerals and quantities.

Sketches: Teach children to sketch their math thinking rather than drawing in detail. For example, ask students to pretend that color disks are flowers, and then ask them to sketch a circle for each flower rather than drawing the details of each flower. You may want to ask them to draw circles or x's to represent quantities as a general rule of thumb. Furthermore, you will serve your students well by asking them to sketch the counters or linking cubes they use for any activity, creating a record of their activity.

Hundred Charts: Although horizontal number tracks are best for children in Grades K–1, students in Grades 2–5 will benefit greatly from using hundreds charts to support their understanding of tens and ones. With much practice, they will begin to understand that horizontal moves "count by ones" and vertical moves "count by tens."

Symbolic Representations

Vertical Number Lines: When the counting sequence is written vertically, children are able to view the pattern of the count, both when counting by ones and when skip counting, either top to bottom or bottom to top. This format supports students in seeing the digit patterns as numerals get increasingly larger. For example, students can see that 0–9 repeat in the ones place as they move up into each decade and that there are ten 1s, ten 2s, ten 3s, and so on, in the tens place. In second grade, this pattern can be built all the way to 1,000. Vertical number lines are often recorded on a roll of cash register tape, unrolling the paper as you go. You can also use a reproducible and have students cut the strips. See Object 5.1 for an example.

> To download the Pattern of the Count Reproducible, visit the companion website at resources.corwin.com/mathsmallgroups.

Numeral Cards: Have students place simple numeral cards next to each set of objects they count. Consider the number set you're working with at the time to help you determine which numeral cards to make available. For example, if kindergarteners are working on quantities through 20, you might give them a set of 1–20 numeral cards. However, if students are working with larger quantities, you may want to give them blank strips of paper so they can write their own numerals.

Objects 5.5 and 5.6 · *Quantities With Numeral Cards*

Verbal Representations

Verbal Counting: You will especially want to ask students to count aloud as they count a set of objects. Then, once they are finished, follow up by asking, "How many are there altogether?" to check if they understand that the last number said in the counting sequence identifies the number of objects in the set. A great way to support counting is to ask students to "see it–say it–touch it," where they actually move each counter as they say the corresponding number. If students are counting objects on a piece of paper, you may want to have them mark each object with a pencil or marker as they say the corresponding number.

Verbal Explanations: When your students are working on their counting skills, ask them to explain and describe their counting. Here are some prompts to use:

- How many . . . ?
- How do you know?
- Can you count them a different way?
- Prove it to me.

Written Explanations: Because of limited literacy skills, young students and students with special learning needs will likely use written explanations less often than in other grade levels. That said, encourage them to record their counting experiences using estimated spelling, more commonly called invented spelling, or other levels along the developmental writing continuum using the same prompts included previously:

- How many . . . ?
- How do you know?
- Can you count them a different way?
- Prove it to me.

Keep in mind that older students would benefit from answering these questions with larger number sets.

Contextual Representations

Teacher-Created Context Problems: Most State Standards Frameworks include context as a way for students to think about their counting experiences. Whenever possible, create a counting experience that includes a high-interest topic. Then ask your students to pretend the counters are _____ (cats, cookies, cars, trees, etc.). This is a great precursor to using variables in later years. For older students who may be counting groups of tens or hundreds, use groupable objects such as boxes of markers or bags of beans.

Student-Created Context Problems: Students benefit tremendously from creating their own counting contexts. This can bring a bit of playfulness into the group, allowing students to make their own connections between math and the real world. Again, ask students to pretend the counters are _____, encouraging them to fill in the blank with their own ideas.

Recording Materials

Provide a variety of recording materials for students to use, including blank paper, dry-erase boards, markers, colored pencils, pencils, and erasers. You may also record student work by taking pictures or videos as they work.

IDENTIFY STRENGTHS: SAMPLE PROMPTS FOR DETECTING LEARNERS' CONTENT STRENGTHS

Step 2 in the small group framework is identifying strengths. In Counting and Cardinality, this includes finding out what students already know about the counting sequence, representing and counting objects, and writing the corresponding numerals. Because this domain usually appears in the early grades, we often overlook the necessity of revisiting these ideas as number sets increase. It will be important to continue similar activities as number sets increase to 100, 1,000, and 1,000,000, and to decimal fractions with digits to the right of the decimal point.

Keep in mind that identifying strengths includes a focus on both you and your students.

1. **Identify teacher strengths.** What do you know about Counting and Cardinality with the number sets your students need to focus on? What strategies will you use to encourage and support students? What do you know about the math content before and after your grade level? How will you support students in connecting out-of-level standards back to your grade-level expectations?

2. **Identify learner strengths.** Use the formative data you've collected as well as the sample prompts that follow to determine learner strengths. What's the last thing they *do* understand along the learning pathway? How do they engage with, represent, and express their learning?

The goal of using these prompts is to identify the last thing the child knows about this particular concept or skill. This will be the starting place for your math small group work, building on successes and connecting to new learning. With the exception of the verbal counting task, you can do these assessment tasks with more than one student at a time by giving them different quantities to count and numeral cards to read.

Count Verbally From "1" (or From Any Number)

The most efficient way for you to determine the last place the child understood the counting sequence is to listen to them count. For each of the following prompts, start by saying, "Start counting at 1 and keep going until I ask you to stop." You can repeat this prompt using other numbers; the key is to make jumps that have the student count across decades and across 100.

- If they get stuck or make a mistake, say "stop" and record how far they made it successfully.

- If they make it to 27 with no hesitation, say "stop" and then ask them to start counting up from 54. If they get stuck or make a mistake, say "stop" and record how far they made it successfully.

- If they make it to 72, say "stop" and then ask them to start counting up from 88. If they get stuck or make a mistake, say "stop" and record how far they made it successfully.

- If they make it to 124, say "stop" and discontinue the assessment. If they get stuck or make a mistake, say "stop" and record how far they made it successfully.

For other number sets, use various starting points to detect if students understand the pattern of the count, especially across benchmark numbers. For example, start counting at 13,993 or start counting at 52.7.

Count Up to 10 Objects Using One-to-One Correspondence and Cardinality

Place seven counters in front of your student in a random arrangement. Ask, "How many counters do you see?" Mark if they correctly demonstrate one-to-one correspondence. Then ask, "How many counters are on the table?" If they state the total without recounting, mark that they demonstrated cardinality. If successful, repeat with 10 counters. If not successful, repeat with five counters.

Counting at this level really is an early primary task. You may ask students to count base-ten objects for other number sets, though that tends to incorporate place value and is included in the place value domain. You can repeat this prompt using other numbers.

Numeral Reading and Writing

Part 1: Show students number cards (0–10 or 0–20) one at a time, and ask them to read the number to you. Part 2: Give each student a piece of paper and pencil or a dry-erase board and marker. Ask them to write the numerals as you say them in random order. Record your students' successes on the recording sheet.

For other number sets, create numeral cards for students to read and write. This is an important skill for large numbers as well as numbers with digits on both sides of the decimal point.

Connecting Quantities, Number Names, and Numerals

Place a set of numeral cards within your selected range in random order on the table. Place a set of objects in front of the student and have them count the objects and identify the corresponding numeral card. Then, give the student a numeral card and have them count out that number of counters. Here are some examples:

- Place six counters on the table in a random configuration in front of the student. Ask the student to count them out loud, tell you how many, and select the corresponding numeral card. Repeat with other numbers to learn more.

- Show the student one digit card and ask them to count out that many counters *without* saying the number name. At the end, point to the set of counters and ask, "How many are here?" Check to see if they can tell you the number without recounting.
- Record your students' successes on the recording sheet.

Again, this skill tends to be isolated in the early primary years. Larger number sets and decimal fractions tend to be included in the place value domain.

CREATE PATHWAYS: SAMPLE TEACHER-FACILITATED SMALL GROUP LESSONS

When creating learning pathways, consider what you've learned about student strengths as starting points to build upon. For example, if students are counting fluently to 10, use that knowledge to build an understanding of the teen numbers.

The three components for Creating Pathways are the following:

▸ Use the Eb4E Lesson Planning Template to plan your lesson.

▸ Consider what you learned about your students' strengths—what do they already know about Counting and Cardinality?

▸ Connect Counting and Cardinality concepts between your math small group work and whole-class learning. Use Counting and Cardinality routines in both settings to help students make connections.

To download the Eb4E Lesson Planning Template, visit resources.corwin.com/mathsmallgroups.

The following selected sample lessons provide examples for how you might design a math-targeted small group lesson, attending to each area of the framework. Note that these examples are written for younger students but can be easily adapted for students working with larger number sets.

ACTIVITY 5.1

The Big Thumb: Counting Up and Back

Focus on Math: In this activity, students connect the verbal counting sequence to the current grade-level content.

Identify Student Strengths: Prior to this activity, identify students' counting strengths by using the "Count Verbally From '1' (or Any Number)" prompt (p.83) or something similar.

Materials:

- None

Create Pathways:

Launch

1. **The Big Thumb:** Ask students to count together, starting at a given number. Give students a thumbs-up each time you want them to count up to the next number. Hold your hand out, palm forward, when you want them to stop. You may also give them a thumbs-down if you want them to count backwards.

2. Start with numbers that the students were generally successful with, and eventually shift toward number sets where they could use some growth.

Explore

1. Have students work in pairs to continue this experience.

2. Assign one to be the counter and the other to be the "big thumb" partner.

3. Call out a start number. The counter in each pair counts up, stops, or counts down based on the gestures of the big thumb partner.

4. **Optional:** Give each pair different start numbers in order to move them into number sets that start with their strengths and push them toward areas of growth.

Discuss

1. As a group, discuss the following questions:
   - How do you know what number comes next?
   - What do you notice about the patterns in the verbal count?
   - How do you know what happens in the twenties, in the forties, and in the sixties?
   - What about in the teen numbers, just after 8, 9, 10?

Wrap Up

1. **Check for Understanding:** Give each student a start number based on their growth point. Ask students to count up from that number until you say stop.

2. **Connect to Grade-Level Content:** Connect counting back to your current whole-class math content. Also, review the verbal counting sequence with the whole class, explicitly connecting it to current grade-level content.

ACTIVITY 5.2

Numeral Reading and Writing

Focus on Math: In this activity, students connect numeral reading and writing to their current grade-level content.

Identify Student Strengths: Prior to this activity, identify students' counting strengths by using the "Numeral Reading and Writing" prompt (p. 84) or something similar.

Materials:

- *Numeral Reading and Writing* (Activity Sheet 5.2), cut out cards ahead of time. Available on the companion website at resources.corwin.com/mathsmallgroups.
- Paper and pencils or dry-erase board and markers

Create Pathways:

Launch

1. Show students one numeral card at a time (0–10), beginning with the numerals that were highly recognized and moving toward the numerals that are growth points.
2. For each card, ask students to name the numeral on the card.
3. Have students "air write" the numerals while looking at one card at a time. They should "write" them with their pointer and middle fingers together, whole arm extended, and then again with just their forefinger extended a little bit.

Explore

1. Place students in pairs, giving each pair a set of numeral cards (0–10) and a set of quantity cards (0–10) to use with the activities that follow.
2. Have students take turns being the "teacher," asking their partners the name of the numbers on the numeral cards and the quantities on the quantity cards.
3. Have each pair work together to place the cards in order from least to greatest.
4. Have students mix up the cards and place them facedown in a pile. Each student uses paper or dry-erase boards to practice writing the numerals as the teacher calls them out.

Discuss

1. Ask students to write the numbers they feel most confident with and then sketch the corresponding quantities.

Wrap Up

1. **Check for Understanding:** Ask students to write numbers, 0–10, as you call them out.

2. **Connect to Grade-Level Content:** Connect numeral reading and writing back to your current whole-class math content. Also, review numeral writing with the whole class, explicitly connecting it to current grade-level content.

Counting Collections

Focus on Math: In this activity, students connect counting principles to current grade-level content.

Identify Student Strengths: Prior to this activity, identify students' counting strengths by using the "Connecting Quantities, Number Names, and Numerals" prompt (p. 84) or something similar.

Materials:

- *Counting Collections* (Activity Sheet 5.3), cut out cards ahead of time. Available on the companion website at resources.corwin.com/mathsmallgroups.
- Blank paper
- Work mat
- Counting collections in small baggies with 4–10 objects in each bag (e.g., beans; cereal bits; pattern blocks; colored pasta; or any kind of small, countable objects)

Create Pathways:

Launch

1. Show students small bags of countable objects. Each bag should have 4–10 objects in it. Examples include beans, cereal bits, or plastic counters.
2. Open one bag and, counting together, determine the quantity of objects in that bag.
3. Record the number on a blank sheet of paper.

Explore

1. Beforehand, have students fold a piece of paper in half, then in half again, to make a simple book. A simple book has eight recording sections, four on the outside and four on the inside.
2. Pass out counting collections, one per student.
3. Have students dump the contents of a bag on a work mat (e.g., piece of craft foam), count the objects, and record the count and a sketch on

one section of the simple book. There are eight spaces on the paper for students to count and record the quantities of eight different sets.

4. Have students take new bags, placing their old ones in the center, for as long as time will allow.

Discuss

1. Ask students the following questions:
   - Which quantities were easier to work with? Why?
   - Are some numbers easier to count than others?
   - Are some numbers easier to get support with than others?
   - How do you know that you're right without asking your teacher or a friend?

Wrap Up

1. **Check for Understanding:** Give each student a new bag of manipulatives. Have them independently and concurrently count, answer the question "How many?," and write the corresponding numeral for their respective counting collections.

2. **Connect to Grade-Level Content:** Connect counting, cardinality, and one-to-one correspondence explicitly to current grade-level content.

YOUR TURN

Throughout this chapter, you had the chance to view math small groups through the lens of the Math Small Group Framework. You focused on the math in the Counting and Cardinality standards, looking at ways to identify strengths and plan for learning pathways. Now it's your turn. Take a moment to reflect on the questions that follow, focusing on how math small groups will benefit the teaching and learning in your classroom.

Learning Intention

After reading this chapter, you will understand how to target the math, identify strengths, and plan pathways for content related to Counting and Cardinality.

Success Criteria

You will be able to use the math content trajectory for Counting and Cardinality, in addition to your State Standards Framework or the *Math Small Group* Standards Trajectory Document, to help you identify the just-right starting place for your students.

The *Math Small Group* Standards Trajectory Document offers a map that shows how all the standards for each domain interrelate. To download this tool, visit resources. corwin.com/mathsmallgroups.

- What ideas did you glean from this chapter that will help you engage in the three steps of the Math Small Group Framework?

- What did you learn about the pathway of Counting and Cardinality across grade levels? How will this help you as you work with your students in the math small group setting?

CHAPTER 6

EARLY NUMBER SENSE

> ## Learning Intention
>
> After reading this chapter, you will understand how to target the math, identify strengths, and plan pathways for content related to Early Number Sense.
>
> ## Success Criteria
>
> You will be able to use the math content trajectory for Early Number Sense, in addition to your State Standards Framework or the *Math Small Group* Standards Trajectory Document, to help you identify the just-right starting place for your students.

CHAPTER INTRODUCTION

Early Number Sense concepts are typically addressed directly in Grades K–2. During those early years, students gain proficiency in composing and decomposing numbers within 20, comparing sets and numerals within 20, and developing fluency for addition and subtraction facts within 20.

Although these concepts are typically considered complete by the end of Grade 2, you may want to consider the implications of these skills with increasingly larger number sets. As students progress through the grade levels, they work on these concepts with numbers within 100 in Grade 1, within 1,000 in Grades 2–3, and within 1,000,000+ in Grades 4–5. In addition, students directly work with numbers that have digits to the right of the decimal point in Grades 4–5.

Although the composing and decomposing and number comparisons at higher levels tend to be included with place value standards, they could be considered extensions of the Early Number Sense domain as well. You may want to consider using the activities in this chapter for larger number sets as all students in Grades K–5 would benefit. Furthermore, continued emphasis on fluency maintenance with addition and subtraction facts within 20 support work with multidigit operations.

EARLY NUMBER SENSE: AN OVERVIEW

Early Number Sense lays an important foundation for all number work to come in later grades. After all, what happens in the ones place happens in every place in the base-ten number system, which further explains why these foundational skills are so important.

First, students compose and decompose numbers within 10, usually partitioning these numbers into pairs. Using part-part-whole charts or number bonds as work mats provides a great way for students to count out a specified number of counters and then explore ways in which they can be partitioned into two subsets. Take care that your students keep all their counters on their work mats when they do this. In addition, partitioning number tracks made of linking cubes also serves as a great way for students to explore different ways a specified number can be composed and decomposed into two subsets.

Next, students compare numbers in two ways. First, they compare the quantities of two sets of objects. This provides a great opportunity for students to visually demonstrate one-to-one correspondence by pairing up the items in each set to see which has "leftovers." Then, once students are proficient with comparing two sets of objects, they compare two numbers presented as written numerals. Success with this skill requires that students have fully connected quantities with number names and numerals, as discussed in Chapter 7 of this book.

Because most State Standards Frameworks include sets of fluency standards, this trajectory concludes with fluency with addition and subtraction within 5. This requires extensive work with the symbols used in equations, specifically +, −, and =. As described in Part A, students often struggle with these symbols when they are introduced too soon. It's important that you give students ample opportunities to understand the actions associated with + and − and that your students understand that the = symbol is a relationship symbol, not an action symbol.

> It's important that you give students ample opportunities
> to understand the actions associated with + and − and
> that your students understand that the = symbol
> is a relationship symbol, not an action symbol.

In Chapter 4, we discussed the Math Small Group Framework. The content in the rest of this chapter will follow the structure of the framework, pictured again in Figure 6.1.

Figure 6.1 · *Teacher-Facilitated Math Small Group Framework*

STEP 1 **Focus on Math**	• Deconstruct grade-level standard(s) of focus • Study the corresponding K-6 standards trajectory • Identify pathway concepts/skills that connect to grade-level standards • Collect formative data based on the learning pathway

STEP 2
Identify Strengths
	• Identify teacher strengths
	• Identify learner strengths
	  ○ What's the last thing students understand along the learning pathway?
	  ○ How do they engage with, represent, and express their learning?

STEP 3 **Create Pathways**	• Use the Explore Before Explain (Eb4E) approach • Ascertain what students *do* know • Connect small group work and whole-class learning in both settings

FOCUS ON MATH: MATH CONTENT TRAJECTORY FOR EARLY NUMBER SENSE

For this first step, Focus on Math, you will want to go through four processes to ensure you identify the necessary content for your students. Although Early Number Sense is primarily an early childhood domain, be sure to account for counting and numeral writing throughout the grade levels, including numerals with digits on both sides of the decimal point. When working with larger numbers, there will be a significant overlap with the place value standards.

The four processes to engage in as you Focus on Math are as follows:

1. Identify and deconstruct the grade-level standard(s) relevant to Early Number Sense.

2. Study the Early Number Sense standards trajectory in this chapter (see Figure 6.2) as well as in the *Math Small Group* Standards Trajectory Document.

3. Identify the multigrade-level pathway concepts and skills that connect to on-grade-level standards for Early Number Sense. This may

include standards from previous grade levels as well as standards for future grade levels. Use whichever standards you need based on the structure (heterogeneous, Guided Math, etc.) and goals for your math small groups.

4. Collect formative data based on the Early Number Sense standards. Your formative data may include daily entrance or exit tickets, weekly common formative assessments, classroom observational data, or any other data you collect on a regular basis.

> The *Math Small Group* Standards Trajectory Document offers a map that shows how all the standards for each domain interrelate. To download this tool, visit resources. corwin.com/mathsmallgroups.

Figure 6.2 · *Trajectory for Early Number Sense*

| Compose and decompose numbers within 10 into pairs | Compare numbers presented as sets of objects | Compare numbers presented as written numerals | Add and subtract within 5 (fluency standard) | Add and subtract within 10 (fluency standard) | Add and subtract within 20 (fluency standard) |

As you saw with the Counting and Cardinality trajectory, the concepts in the Early Number Sense trajectory include content similar to what appears in the place value and operations standards from later grades. Students are composing and decomposing numbers, comparing quantities, and comparing numerals within 10 and within 20 in kindergarten. They will continue working on these same concepts in Grades 1–5, only with different number sets. Again, students apply these skills to numbers within 100 in Grade 1, numbers within 1,000 in Grades 2–3, and numbers within 1,000,000+ in Grades 4–5. Students also work with digits to the right of the decimal point in Grades 4–5. Therefore, the ideas and activities in this chapter might serve you well with students across Grades K–5.

Furthermore, your students work on fluency with addition and subtraction within 5, 10, and 20 in Grades K–2. That said, students in Grades 3–5 benefit tremendously from continued exposure to these basic facts, applying them frequently in multidigit operations. Examine the *Math Small Group Standards Trajectory Document* to learn more about the connections across grade levels.

Algebraic Thinking and Overarching Structures

This math content trajectory includes several overarching themes. These don't generally fall in a specific place along the trajectory. Rather, they appear in several places along the learning continuum, both within and across grade levels. Often, these standards can be used to connect big ideas across domains and grades because they appear so frequently.

Patterns and Generalizations

Continuing the work with the pattern of the count from the previous chapter is very helpful for students when they begin working with Early Number Sense. Continue reinforcing the understanding that the ones place repeats 0–9 while the tens place reveals ten 1s, then ten 2s, then ten 3s, and so forth. Another important skill is mentally identifying one more and one less in the early grades.

Probably the most important idea, though, is for students to discover the patterns that exist when decomposing quantities into number pairs. By simply creating a table or an organized list, students can begin to see that as one addend increases, the other decreases. You can facilitate this understanding frequently using prompting and probing questions such as the following:

- What are different ways to make 5?
- How many different ways did you find?
- Are there any other ways to make 5?
- Can you find a way to organize all the different ways to make 5?
- Do you see any patterns with all the different ways to make 5?

Place Value

What happens in the ones place happens in every place. This makes composing and decomposing 10 into number pairs an important component of this trajectory. In fact, many State Standards Frameworks list this component separate from the rest because it is so important for students to know all of the number pairs that add to 10. Be sure you give your students many opportunities to internalize this idea.

Properties

Although informal, your students will be introduced to the idea of the commutative property during this trajectory as well. For example, as they decompose 10 into its number pairs, they will encounter the idea that as one number increases, the other decreases. Therefore, they will encounter 1 + 9 and 9 + 1 as number pairs. Young students need not call this the commutative property, but you certainly should draw their attention to it.

In addition, young children also encounter "Zero the hero" in their math work. Although they do not formally learn about the identity property at this level, they can and should explore the special properties of zero.

Strategies and Representations

Be sure students have plenty of opportunities to work with multiple representations, as described in the opening section of this chapter. They should especially use these representations when solving context problems that reflect different situation types, including add to, put together, take from, compare, and part-part-whole. You can learn more about problem situation types in the *Mathematize It!* book series from Corwin.

> You can learn more about problem situation types in the *Mathematize It!* book series from Corwin.

MATH TOOLS TO SUPPORT THIS TRAJECTORY

When preparing for teacher-facilitated math small groups, you may be planning for math concepts and skills that are not necessarily at your grade level. The suggestions in this section are intended to help you think through the materials you may need, especially for facilitating conceptual development. As mentioned in Chapter 3, having your materials at your fingertips will protect your small group time from interruptions to collect needed materials.

As you gather materials, be mindful that you include a wide variety so as to encourage students to translate within and across the different categories of representations: concrete (manipulatives and objects), visual, symbolic, verbal, and contextual (Lesh et al., 1987). You should encourage students to represent their thinking in ways that make sense to them, giving them choice as much as possible. In addition, ask students to work side by side with different representations and then compare and contrast what they see. This will help students make sense of their thinking as well as develop new ways of thinking about the concepts and skills at hand.

See Chapter 2 for more information about the Lesh
Translation Model of Representations.

Concrete Representations

Counters: Any small, countable objects will suffice such as round color counters,
unit squares, cereal bits, beans, and so on.

Linking Cubes: Cubes that link together may be used as number tracks. Although
number lines are a common visual used across grade levels, young children
frequently confuse the tick marks rather than the number of "jumps," or spaces
between the tick marks, as indicating the quantity. Instead, number tracks
may be created using linking cubes, with the number of cubes representing the
quantities (see Object 6.1).

Object 6.1 · *Number Track and Linking Cubes Number Lines*

Visual Representations

Work Mats: Common work mats used at this level include ten frames, five
frames, part-part-whole charts, and number bonds. These work mats can
be preprinted and/or laminated, or students may draw their own. You may
want to do a combination of the two. Students can typically draw a number
bond themselves, whereas it's usually best to preprint ten frames, five frames,
and part-part-whole charts as students find it more difficult to draw them
proportionally.

Object 6.2 • *Ten Frames, Five Frames, Part-Part-Whole Charts, and Number Bonds*

Number Tracks: Number tracks, as described earlier under "Linking Cubes," provide a much more concrete visual for students as opposed to number lines. Your students will benefit from using number tracks rather than number lines during the early school years.

Sketches: Teach students to sketch their math thinking rather than drawing in detail. For example, ask students to pretend that color disks are flowers, and then ask them to sketch a circle for each flower rather than drawing the details of each flower. Furthermore, you will serve your students well by asking them to sketch the counters or linking cubes they use for any activity, creating a record of their activity.

Symbolic Representations

Numerals to Represent Quantities: As frequently as possible, ask students to represent their thinking with numbers, pictures, and words. If students need support with numeral writing, see Chapter 7 for suggestions.

Operations Symbols: Young children may or may not be familiar with the + and − symbols. Prior to introducing these symbols, be sure to give students ample opportunities to understand the actions of addition and subtraction. The primary situations used in the early grades include add to, take from, part-part-whole, and compare. Afford students the opportunities to use manipulatives to represent the actions prior to using the symbols.

Relationships Symbols: In addition to the operations symbols, the relationships symbols, including =, <, and >, are often misunderstood by children. They often think that the = symbol is an action symbol meaning "do something and the answer comes next." A great way to help them rectify this issue is to use a True-False Flash Card activity with them on a regular basis (see Object 6.3). You can do this for any number set and any operation.

Object 6.3 · *True-False Quick Looks*

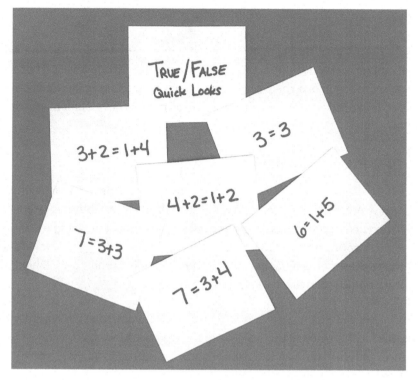

True-False Quick Looks: Write several equations, each on an index card. Examples of true equations include 3 + 2 = 5, 4 = 1 + 3, 8 = 8, and 5 + 4 = 1 + 8. Examples of false equations include 2 + 2 = 7, 5 = 3 + 3, 9 = 10, and 1 + 2 = 3 + 4. Show students one card at a time and ask if the equation is true or false. The main point is that the = sign means both sides represent the same amount. It does *not* mean the answer comes next. Create four or five cards per day, and repeat this activity in small groups or with the whole class two to three times per week. You can use this activity with any number set and any operation, so it's always fresh.

Verbal Representations

Sentence Starters: Think ahead about what kinds of prompts to provide to students to get them talking about math. Create an anchor chart or a set of cards on a binder ring that provide sentence starters. These might include the following:

- I can make [10] with ____ and ____. I know this because . . .
- ____ is greater than ____. I know this because . . .
- ____ is less than ____. I know this because . . .

Verbal Explanations: When students are working on their counting skills, ask them to explain and describe their counting using prompts such as the following:

- How many . . . ?
- How do you know?

- Can you count them a different way?
- Prove it to me.

Written Explanations: Because of limited literacy skills, young students will likely use written explanations less often than in other grade levels. That said, encourage them to record their counting experiences using estimated spelling, often called invented spelling, or other levels along the developmental writing continuum.

Contextual Representations

Teacher-Created Context Problems: Your state standards most likely include context as a way for students to think about their early number experiences. Whenever possible, create a number experience that includes a high-interest topic. Then ask your students to pretend the counters are _____. Thinking about counters as representing objects corresponds to understanding variables as representing numbers in later years.

Student-Created Context Problems: You may also want to ask the students in your targeted math small group to create their own counting context. This can bring a bit of playfulness into the group, allowing students to make their own connections between math and the real world.

Recording Materials

Provide a variety of recording materials for students to use, including blank paper, dry-erase boards, markers, colored pencils, pencils, and erasers.

IDENTIFY STRENGTHS: SAMPLE PROMPTS FOR DETECTING LEARNERS' CONTENT STRENGTHS

Identifying strengths regarding Early Number Sense includes finding out what students already know about composing and decomposing numbers, comparing quantities and numerals, and building fluency with addition and subtraction facts. Because this domain usually appears in the early grades, we often overlook the necessity of revisiting these ideas as number sets increase. You will be wise to continue similar activities as number sets increase to 100, 1,000, and 1,000,000, and to decimal fractions with digits to the right of the decimal point.

Keep in mind that identifying strengths includes a focus on both you and your students.

1. **Identify teacher strengths.** What do you know about Early Number Sense with the number sets your students need to focus on? What strategies will you use to encourage and support students? What do you know about the math content before and after your grade level? How

will you support students in connecting out-of-level standards back to your grade-level expectations?

2. **Identify learner strengths.** Use the formative data you've collected as well as the sample prompts that follow to determine learner strengths. What's the last thing students *do* understand along the learning pathway? How do they engage with, represent, and express their learning?

The goal of using these prompts is to identify the last thing the student knows about this particular concept or skill. This will be the starting place for your math small group work, building on successes and connecting to new learning. With the exception of the verbal counting task, you can do these assessment tasks with more than one student at a time by giving them different quantities to count and numeral cards to read.

Decompose Quantities Into Number Pairs

Have students count out seven objects from a common bucket. Ask students to show you as many ways as possible to decompose seven into two parts. Provide students with blank paper or a part-part-whole mat to record their work. Record student successes and growth points for the following:

- Did they count out seven objects correctly?
- Did they correctly decompose seven into two sets?
- Did they correctly record their decomposition in a way that made sense?
- How did they record their decomposition? Using numbers? Pictures? Organized list? Another way?
- Were they able to explain their thinking?
- Repeat with other numbers as needed.

Compare Numbers Presented as Sets of Objects

Ask students to count out four objects and place them on the left side of their work mats. Then ask them to count out five objects and place them on the right side of their work mats. Ask, "Which shows more, four or five? How do you know?" Record student successes and growth points. You can repeat using other numbers.

Compare Numbers Presented as Numerals

Using a set of 0–10 number cards, set out two cards and ask the student to point to the one that represents more. Ask, "How do you know?" Repeat as needed. Record student successes and growth points.

CREATE PATHWAYS: SAMPLE TEACHER-FACILITATED SMALL GROUP LESSONS

When creating learning pathways, consider what you've learned about student strengths as starting points to build upon. For example, if students are counting fluently to 10, use that knowledge to build an understanding of the teen numbers.

The three components for Creating Pathways are as follows:

- Use the Explore Before Explain (Eb4E) Lesson Planning Template to plan your lesson.
- Consider what you learned about your students' strengths—what do they already know about Early Number Sense?
- Connect Early Number Sense concepts between your math small group work and whole-class learning. Use Early Number Sense routines in both settings to help students make connections.

> To download the Eb4E Lesson Planning Template, visit resources.corwin.com/mathsmallgroups.

The following selected sample lessons provide examples for how you might design a math-targeted small group lesson, attending to each area of the framework. Note that these examples are written for younger students but can easily be adapted for students working with larger number sets.

How Many Ways?

Focus on Math: In this activity, students connect composing and decomposing numbers within 10 into pairs to meet your current grade-level content.

Identify Student Strengths: Prior to this activity, identify students' strengths and growth points by using the "Decompose Quantities Into Number Pairs" prompt (p. 103) or something similar. Use the strengths to connect to new learning.

Materials:

- Two-color counters (each side is a different color)
- *How Many Ways?* (Activity Sheet 6.1), one per group. Available on the companion website at resources.corwin.com/mathsmallgroups.
- Number cards, 2–10
- Various writing materials

Create Pathways:

Launch

1. Place a ten-frame work mat out for each student to explore.
2. Ask, "What do you notice?" "What do you wonder?" "How have you used this before?"
3. Have students place six counters on the ten frame, all with the same color facing up.
4. Have them describe the colors they see that total 6. (Since they only have one color facing up, they should indicate they see six of the same color).
5. Ask, "How could you change just one counter to show 6 another way?" If the students are unsure, suggest they flip over one counter at a time to show the same number, only with two different colors showing.
6. Wait for a student to flip over one counter and say that now there are five of one color and one of the other color. Students will likely then start flipping counters over to find different configurations.

Explore

1. Place the number cards facedown in a pile.
2. Prompt each student or pair of students to flip over one card. That will be the total they place on their ten frame, with each student or pair of students having a different number.

3. Have students play with the two-color counters to find all the different number pairs that total the given number.

4. When each is ready, ask them how they are going to represent their work. Will they sketch pictures? Write numbers? Use paper or dry-erase boards? Allow students to select their recording method and materials.

Discuss

1. Have each student (or student pair) share their recordings with the group, showing how they recorded their decomposed number pairs.

2. As time permits, ask each student (or student pair) to choose a second way of representing their thinking, based on what the others did, and show their own work with a different representation.

Wrap Up

1. **Check for Understanding:** Collect student representations. If they used whiteboards, you can snap a quick photo of each and put it into a digital portfolio.

2. **Connect to Grade-Level Content:** Explicitly connect composing and decomposing quantities into number pairs to your current grade-level content, during both small group and whole-class time.

ACTIVITY 6.2

Which Has More?

Focus on Math: In this activity, students connect comparing numbers presented as sets of objects to your current grade-level content.

Identify Student Strengths: Prior to this activity, identify students' strengths and growth points by using the "Compare Numbers Presented as Sets of Objects" prompt (p. 103) or something similar. Use the strengths to connect to new learning.

Materials:

- Linking cubes
- *Which Has More?* (Activity Sheet 6.2), one per student. Available on the companion website at resources.corwin.com/mathsmallgroups.
- Number cards, 2–10
- Various writing materials

Create Pathways:

Launch

1. Ask students to make two number tracks, one with four cubes and one with five.
2. Ask, "Which one has more? How do you know?"

Explore

1. Distribute a copy of the *Which Has More?* activity sheet to each student.
2. Have students cut apart the cards and place them facedown in a pile.
3. Instruct each student to flip over two cards and make a number track with linking cubes to represent each number shown on the cards.
4. Have students state which one has more and which one has less.
5. Have students repeat this a few times.
6. When ready, challenge each student to decide how to represent their thinking using writing materials.

Discuss

1. Spotlight two or three students' work by asking them to share their numbers and their comparison statement with the group. Also ask them to share their representations.

2. Introduce students to the 1-2-Dot Method for drawing the arrows, if it doesn't come up in conversation.

> **The 1-2-Dot Method:** Write two numbers side by side with a space between them. To compare, draw two dots next to the greater number and one dot next to the lesser number. Then, connect the dots to create an arrow, and the arrow will be facing the correct direction, pointing at the lesser amount. Example:
>
> 23 32

Wrap Up

1. **Check for Understanding:** Flip over two cards and ask students to build two number tracks to represent those numbers.

2. **Connect to Grade-Level Content:** Explicitly connect comparing numbers presented as sets of objects to your current grade-level content, during both small group and whole-class time.

Number Number

Focus on Math: In this activity, students connect comparing numbers presented as sets of numerals to your current grade-level content.

Identify Student Strengths: Prior to this activity, identify students' strengths and growth points by using the "Compare Numbers Presented as Numerals" prompt (p. 103) or something similar. Use the strengths to connect to new learning.

Materials:

- *Number Number* (Activity Sheet 6.3), one per student. Available on the companion website at resources.corwin.com/mathsmallgroups.
- Writing materials

Create Pathways:

Launch

1. Ask each of your students how old they are. If everyone is the same age, ask for a sibling's age.
2. Record two different numbers.
3. Ask students which number is greater and which is lesser. If students are not sure, ask them to draw dots for each underneath the numerals to represent the quantities.
4. *Optional:* If it fits with your small group objective, use the 1-2-Dot Method to write the comparison symbol (<, >, or =).

Explore

1. Distribute a copy of the *Number Number* activity sheet to each student.
2. Have students cut apart the cards and place them facedown in a pile.
3. Instruct each student to flip over two cards, write the numbers, and then write the comparison symbol between them to indicate which one is greater and which is lesser.
4. Have students repeat this a few times.
5. *Optional:* Have students fold a simple book to create eight spaces for recording eight comparisons.

Discuss

1. Spotlight two or three students' work by asking them to share one of their comparison statements with the group.

Wrap Up

1. **Check for Understanding:** Ask each student to flip over two cards and point to the one that is greater. Repeat, asking them to point to the one that is lesser.

2. **Connect to Grade-Level Content:** Explicitly connect comparing numbers presented as sets of numerals to your current grade-level content, during both small group and whole-class time.

YOUR TURN

Throughout this chapter, you had the chance to view math small groups through the lens of the Math Small Group Framework. You focused on the math in the Early Number Sense standards, looking at ways to identify strengths and planning for learning pathways. Now it's your turn. Take a moment to reflect on the following questions, focusing on how math small groups will benefit the teaching and learning in your classroom.

Learning Intention

After reading this chapter, you will understand how to target the math, identify strengths, and plan pathways for content related to Early Number Sense.

Success Criteria

You will be able to use the math content trajectory for Early Number Sense, in addition to your State Standards Framework or the *Math Small Group* Standards Trajectory Document, to help you identify the just-right starting place for your students.

The *Math Small Group* Standards Trajectory Document offers a map that shows how all the standards for each domain interrelate. To download this tool, visit resources.corwin.com/mathsmallgroups.

- What ideas did you glean from this chapter that will help you engage in the three steps of the Math Small Group Framework?

- What did you learn about the pathway of Early Number Sense across grade levels? How will this help you as you work with your students in the math small group setting?

CHAPTER 7

BASE-TEN PLACE VALUE

> ## Learning Intention
>
> After reading this chapter, you will understand how to target the math, identify strengths, and plan pathways for content related to Base-Ten Place Value.
>
> ## Success Criteria
>
> You will be able to use the math content trajectory for Base-Ten Place Value, in addition to your State Standards Framework or the *Math Small Group* Standards Trajectory Document, to help you identify the just-right starting place for your students.

CHAPTER INTRODUCTION

Base-Ten Place Value concepts begin in kindergarten and expand throughout the elementary years. In most State Standards Frameworks, kindergarten students group sets of 11–19 objects into a group of 10 objects and some more. In Grade 1, students group sets of 11–19 objects into one group of 10 and some more. After that, they group objects into tens and ones. Students in Grades 2–3 group objects into hundreds, tens, and ones. Students in Grades 4–5 generalize these groupings as they work with numbers through 1,000,000+ as well as decimal fractions using tenths, hundredths, and thousandths.

Base-Ten Place Value provides a structure on which most future number work is built. It is the foundation for multidigit operations through fifth grade and beyond. Understanding the nesting nature of place value is foundational to conceptual understanding of numbers and operations. Students are best served when they understand three important principles: the relationships between and among the places, the magnitude of each place, and the value represented by digits in each place.

BASE-TEN PLACE VALUE: AN OVERVIEW

In the very beginning, kindergarteners are simply building numbers within 10 and using 10 strategically. Back in Chapter 6, we saw that they are focusing on composing and decomposing 10 into number pairs, preparing for the pattern that will happen in every place when engaging in place-value-based addition and subtraction.

In the case of this trajectory, kindergarteners and first graders are both working with the first group of 10. When representing teen numbers, kindergarteners decompose them into 10 ones and some more ones. However, first graders represent the teen numbers as one group of 10 and some extra ones (see Object 7.1). This may sound very subtle, but it's the first time we see the nesting nature of place value come to life. Ten little ones are nested inside that one group of 10. You can't see them anymore, but they're there.

Object 7.1 • *KP® Ten-Frame Tiles and Base-Ten Blocks Showing Teen Numbers in Both Views*

Typically, first and second graders home in on understanding that two-digit numbers are composed of tens and ones. They should represent two-digit numbers in multiple ways, becoming flexible in their understanding of the nesting that goes on with place value. And they also add mental math to the mix, mentally finding 10 more and 10 less with any two-digit number.

Second and third graders focus on three-digit numbers, once again diving deeply to understand how ones are nested in tens and tens are nested in hundreds. Place value is being learned and used concurrently for operations. Other applications include mentally finding 100 more and 100 less with three-digit numbers as well as adding estimation skills such as rounding.

In Grades 4 and 5, students are introduced to even larger numbers, often going up to six or nine digits as well as adding digits to the right side of the decimal point. Although the word *magnitude* does not tend to be used in the standards, that word embodies the idea that each place has a magnitude that is 10× greater than the place to its right and 1/10 of the place to its left. Essentially, over the course of these six years, we want to make sure that our students understand "place" as the position of the digits, "value" as the value that is assigned to each digit, and magnitude as the relative value of each place.

> We want to make sure that our students understand "place" as the position of the digits, "value" as the value that is assigned to each digit, and magnitude as the relative value of each place.

In Chapter 4, we discussed the Math Small Group Framework. The content in the rest of this chapter will follow the structure of the framework, pictured again in Figure 7.1.

Figure 7.1 · *Teacher-Facilitated Math Small Group Framework*

STEP 1 Focus on Math	• Deconstruct grade-level standard(s) of focus • Study the corresponding K-6 standards trajectory • Identify pathway concepts/skills that connect to grade-level standards • Collect formative data based on the learning pathway

STEP 2
Identify Strengths
	• Identify teacher strengths
	• Identify learner strengths
	  ○ What's the last thing students understand along the learning pathway?
	  ○ How do they engage with, represent, and express their learning?

STEP 3 Create Pathways	• Use the Explore Before Explain (Eb4E) approach • Ascertain what students *do* know • Connect small group work and whole-class learning in both settings

FOCUS ON MATH: MATH CONTENT TRAJECTORY FOR UNDERSTANDING PLACE VALUE

For this first step, Focus on Math, you will want to go through four processes to ensure you identify the necessary content for your students. Base-Ten Place Value spans Grades K–5 and includes both whole numbers and decimal fractions. Consider the connections between Counting and Cardinality and Early Number Sense as you move students through the place value sequence.

The four processes to engage in as you Focus on Math are as follows:

1. Identify and deconstruct the grade-level standard(s) relevant to Base-Ten Place Value.

2. Study the Base-Ten Place Value standards trajectory in this chapter (see Figure 7.2) as well as in the *Math Small Group* Standards Trajectory Document.

3. Identify the multigrade-level pathway concepts and skills that connect to on-grade-level standards for Base-Ten Place Value. This may include standards from previous grade levels as well as standards for future grade levels. Use whichever standards you need based on the structure (heterogeneous, Guided Math, etc.) and goals for your math small groups.

4. Collect formative data based on the Base-Ten Place Value standards. Your formative data may include daily entrance or exit tickets, weekly common formative assessments, classroom observational data, or any other data you collect on a regular basis.

> The *Math Small Group* Standards Trajectory Document offers a map that shows how all the standards for each domain interrelate. To download this tool, visit resources. corwin.com/mathsmallgroups.

Figure 7.2 • *Trajectory for Understanding Place Value*

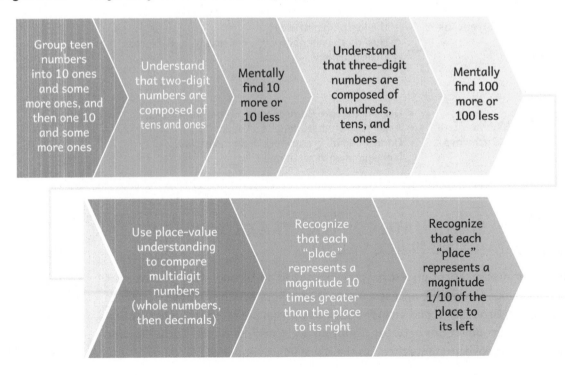

Algebraic Thinking and Overarching Structures

This standards trajectory includes several overarching themes. These don't generally fall in a specific place along the trajectory. Rather, they appear in several places along the learning continuum, both within and across grade levels. Often, these standards can be used to connect big ideas across domains and grades because they appear so frequently.

Patterns and Generalizations

There are many patterns and generalizations inherent in place value to span the grade levels, and they are revisited every time we get to a new number set or a new operation. The first of these is expanded form. Students are first introduced to expanded form in first grade as part of their exploration with two-digit numbers, and it continues through fifth grade with added places to the right-hand side of the decimal point.

Another overarching structure is estimation skills, including rounding. Rounding is included in this chapter because of its close tie to place value. However, estimation includes many different modes and appears in just about every grade level's standards.

Specific to Grades 4 and 5, two new standards emerge: explaining the zero patterns that result when multiplying or dividing by powers of 10 *and* explaining the digit shift patterns around the decimal point when multiplying or dividing by powers of 10.

Across all grades, your students will benefit from thinking about decomposing place value as a pattern-based activity. For example, 124 can be represented as

- ▸ 1 hundred, 2 tens, and 4 ones
- ▸ 12 tens and 4 ones
- ▸ 124 ones

Place Value

Since this chapter is about place value, we won't dwell on this connection too long. Suffice it to say that since place value is one of the most important and prominent structures found in the K–5 math continuum, it will resurface when talking about all four operations and when addressing number sense such as comparing numbers. If learners find themselves struggling with regrouping or decomposing with operations, it may be useful to return to place value concepts. Also important is the development of estimation strategies—be sure to emphasize rounding as one of many estimation strategies, and the one that is most aligned with place value.

Strategies and Representations

The place value trajectory also reminds us that students should be using multiple representations, including objects, sketches, and numbers/equations.

MATH TOOLS TO SUPPORT THIS TRAJECTORY

When preparing for your teacher-facilitated math small groups, you may be planning for math concepts and skills that are not necessarily at your grade level. The suggestions in this section are intended to help you think through the materials you may need, especially for facilitating conceptual development. As mentioned in Chapter 3, having your materials at your fingertips will protect your small group time from interruptions to collect needed materials.

As you gather materials, be mindful that you include a wide variety so as to encourage students to translate within and across the different categories of representations: concrete (manipulatives and objects), visual, symbolic, verbal, and contextual (Lesh et al., 1987). You should encourage students to represent their thinking in ways that make sense to them, giving them choice as much as possible. In addition, ask students to work side by side with different representations and then compare and contrast what they see. This will help students make sense of their thinking as well as develop new ways of thinking about the concepts and skills at hand.

> See Chapter 2 for more information about the Lesh Translation Model of Representations.

Concrete Representations

Base-Ten Manipulatives: Base-ten manipulatives come in two different types: pregrouped and groupable. Although the pregrouped manipulatives are most prominent in our classrooms, the groupable manipulatives are most useful for building student thinking. Base-ten blocks are probably the most prominent base-ten manipulative in classrooms. These simple blocks—which come in units, rods, flats, and cubes—are relatively inexpensive and have been around for nearly a century. Although widely used, they are problematic in that the pieces are pregrouped into what is most commonly identified as tens, hundreds, and thousands. Because they cannot be composed or decomposed, your students must make trades when regrouping from one place to the next.

On the other hand, groupable manipulatives facilitate base-ten thinking in that your students actually compose groups of 10 and nested groups of 10 to represent the true nature of place value. This can be achieved by using linking cubes or bundling straws, or using a tool such as KP® Ten-Frame Tiles, which uses nesting ten frames to allow students to build a group of 10 with 10 ones, a group of 100 with 10 groups of 10, and so on (see Object 7.2).

Object 7.2 • *Different Base-Ten Manipulatives*

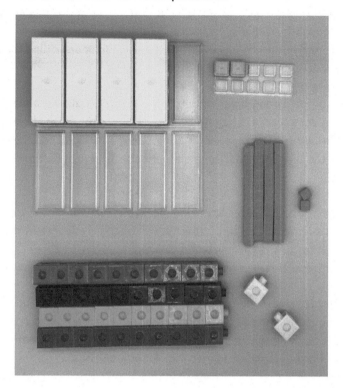

Note that there are many virtual base-ten manipulatives at your disposal, and in that case, even the base-ten blocks may be groupable on the screen.

> For more information on the assets of virtual manipulatives, see *Mastering Math Manipulatives* by Moore and Rimbey (2021).

Counters: Counters may have some limited use at the beginning of place value understanding. However, they become less useful as numbers get larger since they require counting by ones. This is a good property for students to figure out. Encourage students to self-select their math tools. Use prompting and probing questions to help them see that counters are probably not the most appropriate tool to use strategically when working on place value concepts.

Visual Representations

Sketching: Sketching can be a very useful tool for representing numbers as they get incrementally larger on both sides of the decimal point. Using a system that helps students see the patterns within the place values can be very helpful. For example, you may have students use dots in the ones place, lines in the tens place, and squares in the tens place. And then you may have them repeat that pattern for each period.

Period: beginning with the ones place on the right, whole numbers are grouped into three-digit segments, or periods. Each period has a name, such as thousands, millions, and so on. Within each period there is a ones, tens, and hundreds place. The first three digits are called the "units" period.

Place Value Charts: Using place value charts as work mats for place value manipulatives is very useful. They help your students organize their work and scaffold additional information such as the names of the places. They also help students place the blocks in the same sequence as is represented with the digits in the numbers.

Hundreds Charts: Hundreds charts also make terrific work mats for students working on two-digit place value. Students will become experts at detecting patterns related to tens and ones when you use hundreds charts for mental math and other activities.

Open Number Lines: Open number lines can be very helpful to students as they grapple with the magnitude of working with hundreds, tens, and ones. You might consider using a technique where students use different configurations for each kind of "jump." For example, students might draw triangular jumps to represent hundreds, large curved jumps to represent tens, and small curved jumps to represent ones. Some children like to call these "mountains, hills, and pebbles" (see Object 7.3).

Object 7.3 · *Number Line With "Mountains, Hills, and Pebbles"*

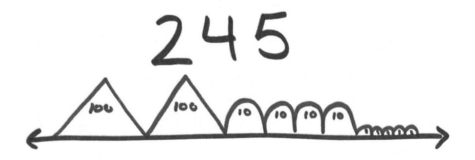

Symbolic Representations

Standard Notation: Students will most frequently write numbers using standard notation. Please note that it is imperative that they develop a sense for the magnitude of each place in the numerals. The fact that each place in a number is 10 times the magnitude of the place to its right, or one-tenth the magnitude of the place to its left, is inherent to the place value system. I like to call this the "nesting nature of place value." Without a full understanding of this principle, your students will misunderstand simple yet important ideas such as regrouping for addition, subtraction, multiplication, and division. Connecting their understanding to concrete and visual representations is an important step for their understanding.

Expanded Notation: When students use expanded notation, they are better able to see the magnitude for each place where the digits reside. You may want to ask students to record numbers using expanded notation more frequently than may be called for in your standards framework or your basal textbook in order to drive this idea home. Also note that, as mentioned in Chapter 6 of this book, the = symbol is often misunderstood as an action symbol rather than as a relationship symbol. Therefore, it is important to remind students through prompting and probing questions and activities such as True-False Flash Cards (see p. 100–101) that it's okay to have the "answer" on either side of the = symbol because it indicates that the value on one side is the same as the value on the other (e.g., 543 = 500 + 40 + 3 or 43 + 5 = 40 + 8). The "answer" need not appear on the right-hand side of the = symbol.

Verbal Representations

Sentence Starters: Think ahead about what kinds of prompts you might provide to your students to get them talking about math. Create an anchor chart or a set of cards on a binder ring that provide sentence starters for your students. Here are a few examples:

> ▸ I know that ____ is the same as ____ because . . .
> ▸ I know that the number ____ has ____ tens and ____ ones because . . .
> ▸ I know that ____ is greater than ____ because . . .

Verbal Explanations: When students are working with place value, ask them to explain and describe the numbers using prompts such as the following:

> ▸ What does this number represent?
> ▸ How do you know?
> ▸ How can you represent the same number in a different way?
> ▸ Prove it to me.

Written Explanations: You may also want to ask students to write about their thinking at different times. Here are two prompts you might want to consider: "What are the steps you used to find your solution?" or "How do you know your solution is correct? Prove it."

Contextual Representations

Teacher-Created Context Problems: Whenever possible, provide context to go along with the numbers with which your students are working. Use people, places, and situations that are of high interest to your students, specifically, or to their age group, generally.

Student-Created Context Problems: Ask students in your math small groups to create their own contexts for the large numbers they're working with. This can bring a bit of playfulness into the group, allowing students to make their own connections between math and their experiences. Especially with place value, encourage students to think about the nesting nature of grouping with tens from one place to the next.

Recording Materials

Provide a variety of recording materials for students to use, including blank paper, dry-erase boards, markers, colored pencils, pencils, and erasers.

IDENTIFY STRENGTHS: SAMPLE PROMPTS FOR DETECTING LEARNERS' CONTENT STRENGTHS

Identifying strengths regarding Base-Ten Place Value includes finding out what students already know about the nesting nature of place value to any place, counting up and down by various benchmarks (e.g., 10 more, 10 less, 100 more, 100 less, 0.1 more, 0.1 less). This work is a continuation of the primary grades with a continued emphasis on comparing numbers, skip counting, and composing and decomposing.

Keep in mind that identifying strengths includes a focus on both you and your students.

1. **Identify teacher strengths.** What do you know about place value with the number sets your students need to focus on? What strategies will you use to encourage and support students? What do you know about the math content before and after your grade level? How will you support students in connecting out-of-level standards back to your grade-level expectations?

2. **Identify learner strengths.** Use the formative data you've collected as well as the following sample prompts to determine learner strengths. What's the last thing students *do* understand along the learning pathway? How do they engage with, represent, and express their learning?

The goal of using these prompts is to identify the last thing the student knows about this particular concept or skill. This will be the starting place for your math small group work, building on successes and connecting to new learning.

Understanding Tens and Ones

Place 17 loose linking cubes in front of each student. Write the number 17. Point to the one and ask the students to show you that many. If they show you a group of 10, then they were successful. If not, ask the students to show you 17 as a group of 10 and some extra ones (see Object 7.4). Notice if they link 10 together and leave 7 ungrouped or if they simply show a group of 10 loose cubes and a group of 7 loose tiles. If they stack together the 10 and then stack together the 7, the results are inconclusive. Record the students' success points from this task. This task can be repeated using any number.

Object 7.4 · *17 Cubes*

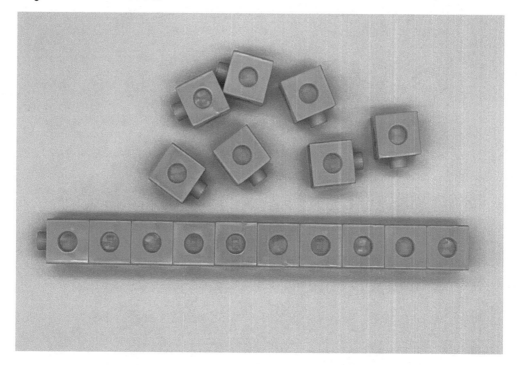

Representing Tens and Ones

Place a bucket of base-ten manipulatives in front of your students. Show them the number 54 and ask them to represent it with the manipulatives (see Object 7.5).

They are successful if they show five groups of 10 and four extra ones. If they don't show that, help them rearrange the manipulatives to show them. Then ask them to show you 54 a different way. Ideally, they'll show four groups of 10 and 14 extra ones, three groups of 10 and 24 extra ones, or some other variation of grouped tens and extra ones that add up to 54. Record your students' successes and growth points. This task can be repeated using any number.

Object 7.5 · *Show 54*

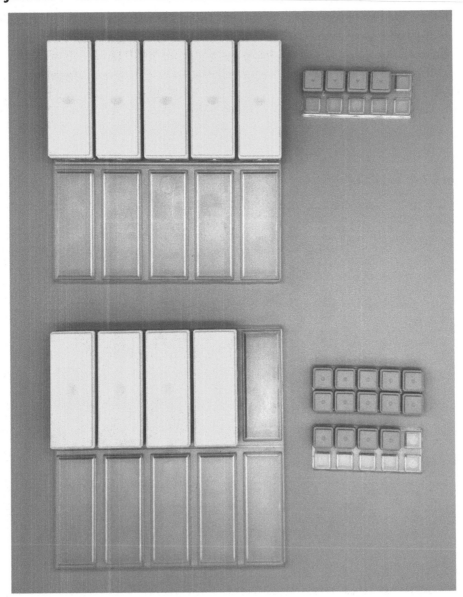

Ten Times More

Ask the student to write the number 444,444. Point to the 4 in the tens place and ask the student to say or write the value of that 4. Point to the 4 in the ten-thousands place and ask the student to say or write the value of that 4. Point to the 4 in the thousands place and ask the student to say or write the value of that 4. Then point to the 4 in the tens place and the 4 in the hundreds place. Ask the student to describe the relationship between those two 4s. Note whether they tell you the value of each and then if they are able to articulate that the 4 in the hundreds place has a value that is 10 times the value of the 4 in the tens place (see Object 7.6). Record your student's successes and growth points. You can repeat using other numbers.

Object 7.6 • *Show 444,444*

"This 4 has a value of 40,000."

"This 4 has a value of 400."

444,444

"Each place has a magnitude that is 10x more than the place to its right."

"This 4 has a value of 400,000."

"This 4 has a value of 40."

CREATE PATHWAYS: SAMPLE TEACHER-FACILITATED SMALL GROUP LESSONS

When creating learning pathways, consider what you've learned about student strengths as starting points to build upon.

The three components for Creating Pathways are as follows:

► Use the Explore Before Explain (Eb4E) Lesson Planning Template to plan your lesson.

► Consider what you learned about your students' strengths—what do they already know about Base-Ten Place Value?

► Connect Base-Ten Place Value concepts between your math small group work and whole-class learning. Use Base-Ten Place Value routines in both settings to help students make connections.

To download the Eb4E Lesson Planning Template, visit resources.corwin.com/mathsmallgroups.

The following selected sample lessons provide examples for how you might design a math small group lesson, attending to each area of the framework. Note that these examples can be easily adapted for students working with all number sets.

Representing Tens and Ones

Focus on Math: In this activity, students connect their understanding of tens and ones to your current grade-level content.

Identify Student Strengths: Prior to this activity, identify students' strengths and growth points by using the "Understanding Tens and Ones" prompt (p. 123) or something similar. Use student strengths to connect to new learning.

Materials:

- *Representing Tens and Ones* (Activity Sheet 7.1). Available on the companion website at resources.corwin.com/mathsmallgroups.
- Counters
- Small portion cups with lids
- Recording materials

Create Pathways:

Launch

1. Distribute a copy of *Representing Tens and Ones* to each student and have them cut apart the cards. Then have students place the cut-apart number cards in a pile facedown.
2. Have students flip over the top card.
3. Ask students to use counters and cups to build that number.
4. Ask prompting and probing questions to help students count out the corresponding number of counters, placing 10 in the cup and leaving the rest loose. Then give them each a lid to cover the group of 10 counters.

Explore

1. Give each student or pair of students a set of counters and a small portion cup with a lid. Also give them a pile of teen cards from *Representing Tens and Ones*.
2. Have students flip over one card and model that number. If needed, ask prompting and probing questions to support them in making a group of 10 and some extra ones.
3. Once successful, have students repeat the activity with another card.

4. When appropriate, have students record their work in the eight sections of a simple book.

5. *Optional:* Stretch those who are ready to represent nonteen two-digit numbers using the same process.

Discuss

1. Lead a discussion of the following questions:
   - What is the connection between the digits in the number and the number of groups-of-10 and extra ones?
   - Is this relationship always true? How do you know?
2. Point to one group of 10 and ask, "How many are here?"
3. Discuss what is similar and what is different about one group of 10 and a group of 10 ones. Using the cups and lids, demonstrate the difference.

Wrap Up

1. **Check for Understanding:** Show your students a teen number and point to the 1. Ask them to show you that many.

2. **Connect to Grade-Level Content:** Explicitly connect understanding tens and ones to your current grade-level content, during both small group and whole-class time.

ACTIVITY 7.2

Race to 100

Focus on Math: In this activity, students connect representing tens and ones to your current grade-level content.

Identify Student Strengths: Prior to this activity, identify students' strengths and growth points by using the "Representing Tens and Ones" prompt (p. 124) or something similar. Use student strengths to connect to new learning.

Materials:

- *Place Value Chart* (Activity Sheet 7.2), one per pair. Available on the companion website at resources.corwin.com/mathsmallgroups.
- Die, one per pair
- Base-ten manipulatives

Create Pathways:

Launch

1. Distribute a *Place Value Chart* to each student.
2. Roll the die and ask students to place that many unit cubes (or whatever represents one) on their *Place Value Charts*.
3. Ask prompting and probing questions as necessary to ensure all students have placed those unit cubes in the ones place.
4. Repeat rolling and placing until there are more than 10. Remind students that whenever they have 10 or more pieces in the ones place, they need to group 10 ones into one group of 10 and place it in the tens place (or trade 10 ones for one rod).

Explore

1. Have students play this game in pairs using the following rules, checking for understanding:
   - Player A rolls the die and places that many units in the ones place (ten-frame formation preferred).
   - Player B rolls the die and adds that many units to the ones place. If there are 10 or more units in the ones place, Player B must regroup the blocks into tens and ones (see Object 7.7).
   - Play continues until the pair reaches 100.

This game can also support the development of base-ten addition. See Chapter 8 for more information on the relationship between place value and addition.

2. Discuss:
   a. How do you know when to regroup?
   b. How many times did you have to regroup by the time you got to 100?
   c. How might you record these ideas on paper?

3. As students play, remind them to stop and look closely if they need to make a group of 10.

4. Students continue playing until they have 10 groups of 10 to trade for one group of 100. If a student finishes early, ask them to either play again or to play *Backwards Race to 0* by starting with a group of 100 and ungrouping as necessary to be able to remove the number of pieces that correspond to the number rolled.

Discuss

1. Ask students why it is important to think of a "10" as a "group of 10" and 100 as a "group of 100." Ten whats? One hundred whats? These can be tough questions to answer—ask prompting and probing questions and use visuals to help students articulate their understandings.

Wrap Up

1. **Check for Understanding:** Show your students the number 37 (or you can show each student a different number). Ask them to represent that number using base-ten manipulatives or sketches. Look for success creating groups of 10 that correspond with the tens digit and leave some extra ones.

2. **Connect to Grade-Level Content:** Explicitly connect "Representing Tens and Ones" to your current grade-level content, during both small group and whole-class time.

Object 7.7 ·

Race to 100

Ten Times More!

Focus on Math: In this activity, students connect their understanding of the notion that "the magnitude of a place in a base-ten number is 10 times more than the place to its right" to your current grade-level content.

Identify Student Strengths: Prior to this activity, identify students' strengths and growth points by using the "Ten Times More" prompt (p. 125) or something similar. Use student strengths to connect to new learning.

Materials:

- *Place Value Chart* (Activity Sheet 7.3a). Available on the companion website at resources.corwin.com/mathsmallgroups.
- *Ten Times More!* (Activity Sheet 7.3b), one per student. Available on the companion website at resources.corwin.com/mathsmallgroups.
- Whiteboards and markers
- Base-ten manipulatives or app

Create Pathways:

Launch

1. Display a three-digit number.
2. Have students represent that number using base-ten manipulatives.
3. Ask students to describe the pieces they used in each place. If students struggle, have them compare the *pieces* in each place—not the number of pieces, but the relative size of the pieces.

Explore

1. Distribute a copy of *Ten Times More!* to each student or pair of students and have them cut apart the cards. Then have students place the cut-apart number cards in a pile facedown.
2. Have students flip over the top card and build that number.
3. Instruct students to compare and contrast the relative size of the pieces they use in each place.
4. Repeat several times, helping students to refine their description each time.

Discuss

1. As a group, discuss the relative size of the pieces used in each place.

2. At the end of the discussion, draw the conclusion that just as the pieces are 10 times the size of the pieces used in the place to the right, this is true of the magnitude of the places when a three-digit number is written in standard form. You may also want to illustrate this idea with expanded form.

Wrap Up

1. **Check for Understanding:** Show students the number 333. Point to the 3 in the tens place and the 3 in the ones place and ask students to describe the relationship between those values. Repeat with other numbers as needed (222, 444, 555, etc.).

2. **Connect to Grade-Level Content:** Explicitly connect the notion of the magnitude of the places in a base-ten number to your current grade-level content, during both small group and whole-class time.

YOUR TURN

Throughout this chapter, you had the chance to view math small groups through the lens of the Math Small Groups Framework. You focused on the math in the Place Value standards, looking at ways to identify strengths and planning for learning pathways. Now it's your turn. Take a moment to reflect on the following questions, focusing on how math small groups will benefit the teaching and learning in your classroom.

Learning Intention

After reading this chapter, you will understand how to target the math, identify strengths, and plan pathways for content related to Base-Ten Place Value.

Success Criteria

You will be able to use the math content trajectory for Base-Ten Place Value, in addition to your State Standards Framework or the *Math Small Group* Standards Trajectory Document, to help you identify the just-right starting place for your students.

The *Math Small Group* Standards Trajectory Document offers a map that shows how all the standards for each domain interrelate. To download this tool, visit resources. corwin.com/mathsmallgroups.

- What ideas did you glean from this chapter that will help you engage in the three steps of the Math Small Group Framework?
- What did you learn about the pathway of Base-Ten Place Value across grade levels? How will this help you as you work with your students in the math small group setting?

CHAPTER 8

BASE-TEN ADDITION AND SUBTRACTION

> ## Learning Intention
>
> After reading this chapter, you will understand how to target the math, identify strengths, and plan pathways for content related to Base-Ten Addition and Subtraction.
>
> ## Success Criteria
>
> You will be able to use the math content trajectories for Base-Ten Addition and Subtraction, in addition to your State Standards Framework or the *Math Small Group* Standards Trajectory Document, to help you identify the just-right starting place for your students.

CHAPTER INTRODUCTION

Base-Ten Addition and Subtraction concepts begin in first grade and expand throughout the elementary years. In most State Standards Frameworks, first- and second-grade students conceptually work on addition and subtraction with two-digit numbers, and third- and fourth-grade students conceptually work on addition and subtraction with three-digit numbers. Whole-number addition and subtraction are formalized with the standard algorithm by fourth grade. In addition, fourth- and fifth-grade students conceptually work on addition and subtraction with decimal fractions.

Base-Ten Addition and Subtraction rely heavily upon a strong foundation of place value. Understanding the nesting nature of place value is foundational to the notion of regrouping (grouping for addition and ungrouping for subtraction). Students are best served when they understand the relationship between place value and its application in multidigit addition and subtraction.

BASE-TEN ADDITION AND SUBTRACTION: AN OVERVIEW

When planning for a focus on addition and subtraction, understanding the trajectories across grades can help you pinpoint the just-right learning pathways for your students.

The addition and subtraction trajectories typically begin in kindergarten with composing and decomposing numbers within 10. This work is often done with concrete objects using structures such as number bonds or part-part-whole charts. Students can engage in the actions of putting together and taking apart prior to a formal introduction to the related symbols. Additional time should be spent working on composing and decomposing the number 10 since this is foundational for place-value-based addition and subtraction. Again, what happens in the ones place happens in every place.

As students move toward a more formalized study of addition and subtraction, ensuring they clearly understand the symbols + and – as action or comparison symbols is critical. Even more so, students need to understand that the = symbol represents a relationship between the expressions on either side. You may want to revisit the True-False Quick Looks from Chapter 6 on occasion, using different number sets as your students move along these trajectories. In addition, you will want to tap into the plethora of thinking strategies available to students, including counting on, making 10, using doubles, using near-doubles, adding 10, adding 9 and "pretend-a-10" (see Figure 8.1). These specific strategies, when you introduce them well, can provide a fantastic means for students to internalize what we often refer to as "the basic math facts." To learn more about these and other strategies, check out *Figuring Out Fluency in Mathematics Teaching and Learning* by Bay-Williams and SanGiovanni (2021).

> To learn more about these and other strategies, check out *Figuring Out Fluency in Mathematics Teaching and Learning, Grades K-8*, by Bay-Williams and SanGiovanni (2021).

Figure 8.1 • *Common Addition and Subtraction Fact Strategies*

> ➢ Count On/Back 1, 2, 3
> ➢ Doubles and Near Doubles
> ➢ Make-a-10
> ➢ Pretend-a-10
> ➢ Add-a-10
> ➢ Think Addition (to subtract)

Next in the addition and subtraction trajectories, you see that students must understand the relationship between addition and subtraction. This does not necessarily happen at one point in time. Rather, it's something that evolves, usually as students are working on addition and subtraction within 20. This may look like thinking about subtraction as a missing-addend problem or "counting up" from the subtrahend to the minuend to find the difference. This basic structure of inverse operations will follow students throughout their algebra trajectory, so focusing on it now is critical.

The next three stops along the trajectories simply show that students are working with increasing number sets. Note that when working with one-, two-, and three-digit numbers, students should develop their understanding conceptually prior to working with the standard algorithms. Typically, many State Standards Frameworks reserve the standard algorithms for Grades 3 or 4, allowing ample opportunities for students to develop full understanding of the actions for addition and subtraction. Some of the conceptual strategies students may use, partially mentioned earlier, may include those shown in Figure 8.2.

Figure 8.2 • *Common Conceptual Addition and Subtraction Strategies*

✓ Count On/Count Back
✓ Make Tens
✓ Partial Sums and Differences
✓ Compensation
✓ Think Addition

In Chapter 4, we discussed the Math Small Group Framework. The content in the rest of this chapter will follow the structure of the framework, pictured again in Figure 8.3.

Figure 8.3 • *Teacher-Facilitated Math Small Group Framework*

STEP 1 **Focus on Math**	• Deconstruct grade-level standard(s) of focus • Study the corresponding K-6 standards trajectory • Identify pathway concepts/skills that connect to grade-level standards • Collect formative data based on the learning pathway

STEP 2
Identify Strengths
	• Identify teacher strengths
	• Identify learner strengths
	  ○ What's the last thing students understand along the learning pathway?
	  ○ How do they engage with, represent, and express their learning?

STEP 3 **Create Pathways**	• Use the Explore Before Explain (Eb4E) approach • Ascertain what students *do* know • Connect small group work and whole-class learning in both settings

FOCUS ON MATH: MATH CONTENT TRAJECTORIES FOR BASE-TEN ADDITION AND SUBTRACTION

For this first step, Focus on Math, you will want to go through four processes to ensure you identify the necessary content for your students. Base-Ten Addition and Subtraction spans Grades K–5 and includes both whole numbers and decimal fractions.

The four processes to engage in as you Focus on Math are as follows:

1. Identify and deconstruct the grade-level standard(s) relevant to Base-Ten Addition and Subtraction.

2. Study the Base-Ten Addition and Subtraction standards trajectories in this chapter (see Figure 8.4) as well as in the *Math Small Group Standards Trajectory Document*.

3. Identify the multigrade-level pathway concepts and skills that connect to on-grade-level standards for Base-Ten Addition and Subtraction. This may include standards from previous grade levels as well as standards for future grade levels. Use whichever standards you need based on the structure (heterogeneous, Guided Math, etc.) and goals for your math small groups.

4. Collect formative data based on the Base-Ten Addition and Subtraction standards. Your formative data may include daily entrance or exit tickets, weekly common formative assessments, classroom observational data, or any other data you collect on a regular basis.

Figure 8.4 • *Trajectories for Base-Ten Addition and Subtraction*

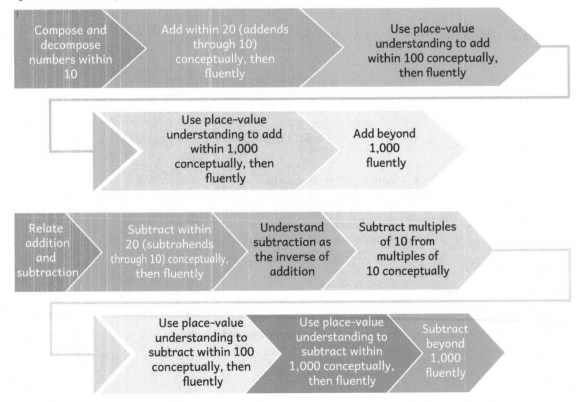

Algebraic Thinking and Overarching Structures

In addition to the specific standards listed on the trajectory maps, the addition and subtraction standards trajectories include several overarching themes as well. They don't generally fall in a specific place along the trajectories; rather, they appear in several places along the learning continuum, both within and across grade levels. Often, these standards can be used to connect big ideas across domains and grades because they appear so frequently.

Patterns and Generalizations

Although the notion of inverse operations was mentioned previously, it's worth noting again here since it provides such a strong connection across grade levels, all the way up into algebra. You will want to keep strategies based on the relationship between addition and subtraction at the forefront of your students' work, especially when engaging with subtraction.

Another generalization is that of using estimation strategies, including rounding, as students assess the reasonableness of their work. This set of strategies often gets reduced to rounding because it is directly called out in most standards documents. However, there are a plethora of estimation strategies students can rely on (see Figure 8.5).

Figure 8.5 · *Estimation Strategies*

❏ Rounding (only one of many strategies)
❏ Benchmark Numbers
❏ Chunking
❏ Front-End Estimation

Place Value

As listed in the previous section, there are many place-value-based strategies students can use to demonstrate conceptual understanding of addition and subtraction. These strategies, combined with those based on the properties of operations and the relationship between addition and subtraction, should comprise the majority of multidigit arithmetic work through third grade, typically through three-digit numbers. It's usually around fourth grade where the standard algorithms for even larger number addition and subtraction are introduced.

Properties

Students should become fluent with using the commutative, associative, and identity properties of addition. The goal of this work is not to define the properties, but rather to use them to make addition easier. A common misconception is that these properties hold true for subtraction, which is not true in the way we teach subtraction in the elementary years. Once students begin working with negative integers, usually around sixth grade, they will gain deeper insight for how the properties interact with subtraction using inverse operations. For now, students must internalize that the properties only belong to addition.

Strategies and Representations

The representations listed in many State Standards Frameworks, beginning in kindergarten and continuing throughout the elementary years, include using objects, fingers, mental images, drawings, sounds, acting-out situations, verbal explanations, expressions, and equations. You can see a more thorough analysis in the opening section of this chapter.

For word problems, include a variety of word problem situations as you arrive at each new number set (see Figure 8.6). Generally, students should engage in word problem situations that include join, separate, part-part-whole, and compare situations. And they should regularly solve problems where the missing number is not always the answer; rather, the missing number should appear in different places within the word problems.

> For more ideas regarding word problem situations, check out the *Mathematize It!* book series from Corwin.

Figure 8.6 · *Word Problem Types for Addition and Subtraction*

Addition and Subtraction Situations

	Result Unknown	Change Addend Unknown	Start Addend Unknown
Add to	Nancy has 4 cookies and Deb gives her 8 more. How many cookies does Nancy have altogether?	Nancy has 4 cookies. How many more does she need to have 12 cookies?	Nancy has some cookies. Deb gives her 8 more cookies, and now she has 12 cookies. How many did she have to start with?
Take From	Nancy has 12 cookies. She gives 4 to Deb. How many cookies does Nancy have now?	Nancy has 12 cookies. She gives some to Deb. Now Nancy has 4 cookies left. How many did she give to Deb?	Nancy has some cookies. She gives 8 to Deb. Now she has 4 left. How many cookies did Nancy have to start with?
Part-Part-Whole	(Total Unknown) Nancy has 4 vanilla cookies and 8 chocolate chip cookies. How many cookies does she have?	(One Part Unknown) Nancy has 4 vanilla cookies and the rest are chocolate chip. She has 12 cookies in all. How many chocolate chip cookies does she have?	(Both Parts Unknown) Nancy has 12 cookies. Some are vanilla and some are chocolate chip. How many of each might she have?

Additive Comparison	(Difference Unknown) Nancy has 12 cookies and Deb has 8 cookies. How many more cookies does Nancy have than Deb?	(Greater Quantity Unknown) Nancy has 4 more cookies than Deb. Deb has 8 cookies. How many cookies does Nancy have?	(Lesser Quantity Unknown) Nancy has 4 more cookies than Deb. Nancy has 12 cookies. How many cookies does Deb have?

And finally, when writing an equation to represent the word problem situation, students should use a symbol to represent the missing number. Many State Standards Frameworks expect that beginning somewhere around third grade, this symbol will be a letter. When students are reading the expressions and equations, be sure they are reading for meaning rather than simply reading the symbols. For example, when looking at $12 + 17 = f$, they might say, "12 and 17 put together is the same value as a number we're calling f."

> **Fun fact:** When using letters as variables, we conventionally use lowercase letters for algebra (including arithmetic) and uppercase letters for geometry.

MATH TOOLS TO SUPPORT THESE TRAJECTORIES

When preparing for your teacher-facilitated math small groups, you may be planning for math concepts and skills that are not necessarily at your grade level. The suggestions in this section are intended to help you think through the materials you may need, especially for facilitating conceptual development. As mentioned in Chapter 3, having your materials at your fingertips will protect your small group time from interruptions to collect needed materials.

As you gather materials, be mindful that you include a wide variety to encourage students to translate within and across the different categories of representations: concrete (manipulatives and objects), visual, symbolic, verbal, and contextual (Lesh et al., 1987). You should encourage students to represent their thinking in ways that make sense to them, giving them choice as much as possible. In addition, ask students to work side by side with different representations and then compare and contrast what they see. This will help students make sense of their thinking as well as develop new ways of thinking about the concepts and skills at hand.

> See Chapter 2 for more information about the Lesh Translation Model of Representations.

Concrete Representations

Base-Ten Manipulatives: Base-ten manipulatives come in two different types: pregrouped and groupable. Please see the conversation at the beginning of Chapter 7. When regrouping for addition and subtraction, using groupable manipulatives is highly preferred, if possible. Although base-ten blocks are widely used, they are problematic in that the pieces are pregrouped into what is most commonly identified as tens, hundreds, and thousands, and because they cannot be composed or decomposed, your students must make trades when regrouping from one place to the next. This does not mirror the place value system, where magnitudes of ten are "nested" inside rather than separate entities. In order to add or subtract unlike magnitudes, we must ungroup in order to make like magnitudes.

Counters: Counters may have some limited use to support understanding at the beginning of place-value-based addition and subtraction. However, they become less useful as numbers get larger since they require counting by ones, which is not realistic as numbers increase in size.

Visual Representations

Sketching: Sketching can be a very useful tool for representing numbers as they get incrementally larger. Using a system that helps students see the patterns within the place values can also be very useful. For example, you may have students use dots in the ones place, lines in the tens place, and squares in the hundreds place. And then you may have them repeat that pattern for each period.

Place Value Charts: As mentioned in Chapter 7, using place value charts as work mats for place value manipulatives is very helpful. They help your students organize their work, scaffold additional information such as the names of the places, and place the blocks in the same sequence as is represented with the digits in the numbers.

Hundreds Charts: Hundreds charts also make terrific work mats for younger children working on two-digit addition and subtraction. Students will become experts at detecting patterns related to adding and subtracting tens and ones when you use hundreds charts for mental math and other activities.

Open Number Lines: Open number lines can be very helpful for students as they grapple with adding and subtracting hundreds, tens, and ones. You might consider using a technique where students use different configurations for each kind of "jump." For example, students might draw triangular jumps to represent hundreds, large curved jumps to represent tens, and small curved jumps to represent ones. Some students like to call these "mountains, hills, and pebbles" (see Object 8.1).

Object 8.1 · *Number Line With "Mountains, Hills, and Pebbles"*

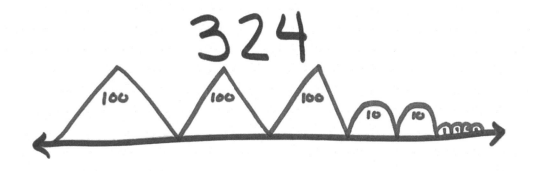

Symbolic Representations

Standard Notation: Students frequently write numbers using standard notation to add and subtract. Please note that it is imperative that they develop a sense for the magnitude of each place in the numerals, knowing that they will need to add and subtract like magnitudes. Connecting their understanding to concrete and visual representations is an important step for their conceptual understanding.

Standard Algorithms: Quite often, we introduce standard algorithms far too soon in the learning sequence. Many State Standards Frameworks expect that students do not use standard algorithms for addition and subtraction until third or fourth grade. Before then, students should use conceptual strategies based on place value, properties of operations, and the relationship between addition and subtraction. Students may still use symbolic representations to represent their thinking, but standard algorithm work can wait until later so we can fully develop conceptual understanding beforehand.

Expanded Notation: One conceptual way to approach addition and subtraction that uses symbolic notation is to use the expanded form of numbers to reinforce addition and subtraction of like magnitudes (see Object 8.2). The need for regrouping also becomes transparent.

Object 8.2 · *Expanded Form for Addition and Subtraction*

Expanded Form

Addition	Subtraction
$24 + 37$	$57 - 34$
$20 + 4 + 30 + 7$	$(50 + 7) - (30 + 4)$
$50 + 11 = 61$	$20 + 3 = 23$

Verbal Representations

Sentence Starters: Think ahead about what kinds of prompts you might provide to your students to get them talking about addition and subtraction. Create an anchor chart or a set of cards on a binder ring that provides sentence starters for your students. Examples include the following:

▸ I will use the make-a-10 strategy when adding ____ and ____ because . . .

▸ I know I will have to group-a-10 when adding ____ and ____ because . . .

▸ I know I will have to ungroup-a-10 when subtracting ____ and ____ because . . .

Verbal Explanations: When your students are working addition and subtraction, ask them to explain and describe their thinking. This might include asking them to whisper-talk to themselves as they describe the steps they're using to add and subtract. Sometimes saying things out loud helps us make sense of our own work or realize where we've made an error in our thinking or calculations.

Written Explanations: You may also want to ask students to write about their thinking at different times. Here are two prompts you might want to consider: "What are the steps you used to find your solution?" or "How do you know your solution is correct? Prove it."

Contextual Representations

Teacher-Created Context Problems: Whenever possible, provide context to go along with the addition and subtraction problems your students are working with. Use people, places, and situations that are of high interest to your students, specifically, or to their age group, generally.

Student-Created Context Problems: You may also want to ask the students in your math-targeted small groups to create their own contexts for the addition and subtraction problems they're working with. You simply provide the expression or equation, and your students compose the word problem. This can bring a bit of playfulness into your small groups, allowing students to make their own connections between math and the real world.

Recording Materials

Provide a variety of recording materials for students to use, including blank paper, whiteboards, markers, colored pencils, pencils, and erasers.

IDENTIFY STRENGTHS: SAMPLE PROMPTS FOR DETECTING LEARNERS' CONTENT STRENGTHS

Identifying strengths regarding Base-Ten Addition and Subtraction includes finding out what students already know about the nesting nature of place value to any place, and counting up and down by various benchmarks (e.g., 10 more, 10 less, 100 more, 100 less, 0.1 more, 0.1 less). This work is a continuation of the primary grades with a continued emphasis on comparing numbers, skip counting, and composing and decomposing.

Keep in mind that identifying strengths includes a focus on both you and your students.

1. **Identify teacher strengths.** What do you know about base-ten addition and subtraction with the number sets your students need to focus on? What strategies will you use to support students? What do you know about the math content before and after your grade level? How will you support students in connecting out-of-level standards back to your grade-level expectations?
2. **Identify learner strengths.** Use the formative data you've collected as well as the following sample prompts to determine learner strengths. What's the last thing students *do* understand along the learning pathway? How do they engage with, represent, and express their learning?

The goal of using these prompts is to identify the last thing the student knows about this particular concept or skill. This will be the starting place for your math small group work, building on successes and connecting to new learning.

Compose and Decompose 10

Given a number between 1 and 9, ask the student to tell you the corresponding number that will go with it to make 10. For example, if you say "three," the student should say "seven." If this is too abstract, set out 10 counters and ask the student to identify three number pairs that make a 10. Record student successes and growth points. You can repeat using other numbers between 1 and 9.

Grouping Tens (and Hundreds) for Addition

Show the student the problem 27 + 35 (or any two two-digit numbers that will require that students group-a-10). Without giving them writing tools, ask them to tell you how they would add these two numbers together. The goal is not to look for a solution, but rather an understanding that the tens go with the tens and the ones go with the ones. If the student struggles to get started, ask prompting and probing questions such as the following:

- Where would you start?
- What do you know about the 2 and the 3?
- What do you know about the 7 and the 5?

This prompt may also be used with three-digit numbers such as 127 + 235. Record student successes and growth points. You can repeat using other numbers.

Connecting Addition and Subtraction

Show the student the equation 15 + 54 = 69 (or any two two-digit numbers that will not require that students group-a-10). Ask them to represent the problem with base-ten manipulatives or sketches, attending to the place value elements for each number. Next, ask the student to show how they could use these numbers to create a subtraction problem using the same numbers. Ask them to use the same base-ten manipulatives or sketches to explain their thinking. Record student successes and growth points. You can repeat using other equations.

Ungrouping Tens (and Hundreds) for Subtraction

Display a card with the number 62 written on it. Ask the student to build that number with base-ten manipulatives. Then ask the student to take away 35. Watch to see how they go about ungrouping a 10 to successfully remove 35. Record student successes and growth points. You can repeat using other numbers.

CREATE PATHWAYS: SAMPLE TEACHER-FACILITATED SMALL GROUP LESSONS

When creating learning pathways, consider what you've learned about student strengths as starting points to build upon.

The three components for Creating Pathways are as follows:

▸ Use the Explore Before Explain (Eb4E) Lesson Planning Template to plan your lesson.

▸ Consider what you learned about your students' strengths—what do they already know about Base-Ten Addition and Subtraction?

▸ Connect Base-Ten Addition and Subtraction concepts between your math small group work and whole-class learning. Use Base-Ten Place Value routines in both settings to help students make connections.

> To download the Eb4E Lesson Planning Template, visit resources.corwin.com/mathsmallgroups.

The following selected sample lessons provide examples for how you might design a targeted-math small group lesson, attending to each area of the framework. Note that these examples can be easily adapted for students working with all number sets.

Fishing for Tens

Focus on Math: In this activity, students connect composing and decomposing a 10 to your current grade-level content.

Identify Student Strengths: Prior to this activity, identify students' strengths and growth points by using the "Compose and Decompose 10" prompt (p. 146) or something similar. Use student strengths to connect to new learning.

Materials:

- *Decks of Cards* (Activity Sheet 8.1), cut out ahead of time. Available on the companion website at resources.corwin.com/mathsmallgroups.
- Ten frames
- Two-color counters

Create Pathways:

Launch

1. Use a ten frame to introduce the idea of number pairs that make 10.
2. Use two-color counters to guide students' thinking.
3. Use that information to teach the students the rules of the game.

Explore

1. Have students play the game in pairs using the following directions:
   - Place cards in a pile facedown.
   - Each student takes 5 cards and holds them so no one else can see them.
   - Students look at their cards and pull out any number pairs that add to 10. Then they draw cards from the pile to ensure they begin the game with 5 cards.
   - One student in the pair asks the other student for a number that pairs with a card in their hand to make a 10. If they are successful, they place the pair of cards in front of them and ask again. Once they ask for a card the other player does not have, their turn is over, and they take one card from the pile. If the card they drew makes a 10 with another card, they place the pair in front of them, and their turn is over.

- Play continues until one person has placed all their cards in pairs.
- The player with the most pairs wins the game.

Discuss

1. Lead a discussion with students using questions such as the following:
   - How many different ways are there to make a 10?
   - Did the same numbers always go together?
   - Can you find a pattern in the number pairs that add to 10?
   - What would be a good way to remember which numbers go together to make a 10?

Wrap Up

1. **Check for Understanding:** Ask students to list number pairs that add to 10.
2. **Connect to Grade-Level Content:** Explicitly connect composing and decomposing a 10 to your current grade-level content, during both small group and whole-class time.

Extension: This game can also be played as Fishing for Hundreds (using cards with numbers 10–90), Fishing for Thousands (using cards with numbers 100–900), or Fishing for Wholes (using cards with numbers 0.1–0.9).

Grouping Tens

Focus on Math: In this activity, students connect grouping tens for addition to your current grade-level content.

Identify Student Strengths: Prior to this activity, identify students' strengths and growth points by using the "Grouping Tens (and Hundreds) for Addition" prompt (p. 146) or something similar. Use student strengths to connect to new learning.

Materials:

- Two dice per pair
- Base-ten blocks *or* KP® Ten-Frame Tiles

Create Pathways:

Launch

1. Show students the problem 27 + 35.
2. Ask them what they know about each number, using prompting and probing questions to lead them to focus on tens and ones.
3. Place base-ten manipulatives within reach and ask them to work together to represent each number.
4. Use prompting and probing questions to support them as they find the sum.
    - Which digits represent groups of 10?
    - Which digits represent ones?
    - Can you show me these numbers with objects or sketches?
    - Why do you put like magnitudes together?
    - Which digits will you put together?

Explore

1. Explain the process for the activity.
    - Player 1 rolls two dice and writes a two-digit number.
    - Player 2 rolls the dice and writes another two-digit number.
    - Each player represents their number with base-ten manipulatives.
    - Player 1 adds the numbers with manipulatives, and player 2 adds the number with symbols.
    - Players switch roles and repeat this process until time is up.

Discuss

1. Ask pairs to explain their work to the group.

2. Use prompting and probing questions such as the following:

   - How do you use place value to know which digits to add together?

   - How do you know when to regroup?

   - How did the base-ten manipulatives help you see what to do?

   - How did you record these ideas on paper?

Wrap Up

1. **Check for Understanding:** Ask students to explain the regrouping process.

2. **Connect to Grade-Level Content:** Explicitly connect grouping tens for addition to your current grade-level content, during both small group and whole-class time.

ACTIVITY 8.3

Connecting Addition and Subtraction

Focus on Math: In this activity, students connect the relationship between addition and subtraction to your current grade-level content.

Identify Student Strengths: Prior to this activity, identify students' strengths and growth points by using the "Connecting Addition and Subtraction" prompt (p. 146) or something similar. Use student strengths to connect to new learning.

Materials:

- Base-ten blocks *or* KP® Ten-Frame Tiles

Create Pathways:

Launch

1. Display the equation 15 + 54 = 69.
2. Ask students how they could use these numbers to show a related subtraction problem.
3. As a group, represent the problem using manipulatives or sketches.
4. Use prompting and probing questions to facilitate a conversation about the relationship between addition and subtraction with these equations. Examples include the following:
   - How are addition and subtraction alike? How are they different?
   - When you add, the sum stands alone. What do you do with that total when you're subtracting?
   - What happens to the addends when you use them to subtract?

Explore

1. Divide students into pairs.
2. Pose the following task: Crystal gathered 15 cucumbers and 54 carrots from her family garden. How many vegetables did she gather altogether?
3. Use base-ten manipulatives, sketches, or a hundreds chart to find the solution.
4. As each pair completes the first task, pose a new one: You already know that Crystal gathered 69 vegetables. If she uses 15 of them for dinner, how many were left? What if she used up 54, how many were left? Have students use base-ten manipulatives, sketches, or a hundreds chart to find the solution.

Discuss

1. Have students share their findings with the group.

2. Use prompting and probing questions to support the conversation, such as the following:

   - How do addition and subtraction relate to one another?

   - How does the sum in an addition equation relate to the "start number" in a related subtraction equation?

   - What happens to the addends when you use them to subtract?

3. Emphasize the relationship between the three numbers used for the addition and subtraction situations.

Wrap Up

1. **Check for Understanding:** Ask students to explain the relationship between addition and subtraction, emphasizing the relationship between the three numbers in the related equations.

2. **Connect to Grade-Level Content:** Explicitly connect ungrouping tens for subtraction to your current grade-level content, during both small group and whole-class time.

Backwards Race to Zero

Focus on Math: In this activity, students connect ungrouping tens for subtraction to your current grade-level content.

Identify Student Strengths: Prior to this activity, identify students' strengths and growth points by using the "Ungrouping Tens (and Hundreds) for Subtraction" prompt or something similar (p. 146). Use student strengths to connect to new learning.

Materials:

- Dice (one die per pair of students)
- Base-ten blocks *or* KP® Ten-Frame Tiles
- *Place Value Chart* (Activity Sheet 8.4). Available on the companion website at resources.corwin.com/mathsmallgroups.

Create Pathways:

Launch

1. Show students a two-digit number.
2. Ask students to use objects to show what it looks like to "unbundle" one group of 10.
3. Discuss how this looks different, but it's still the same amount.

Explore

1. Divide students into pairs to play the game and explain the rules using the following directions:
   - Players start with a filled tile of 100 or a 100-flat on the place value mat.
   - Player A rolls the die and removes that many units in the ones place, ungrouping as needed.
   - Player B rolls the die and removes that many units in the ones place, ungrouping as needed.
   - Play continues until the pair reaches zero. The first pair to get to zero wins the game.

Discuss

1. Use the following questions to discuss the concepts explored in the game:

    - How do you know when to ungroup?

    - How many times did you have to unbundle by the time you got to zero?

    - How might you record these ideas on paper?

Wrap Up

1. **Check for Understanding:** Ask students to explain the regrouping process.

2. **Connect to Grade-Level Content:** Explicitly connect ungrouping tens for subtraction to your current grade-level content, during both small group and whole-class time.

YOUR TURN

Throughout this chapter, you had the chance to view math small groups through the lens of the Math Small Group Framework. You focused on the math in the Base-Ten Addition and Subtraction standards, looking at ways to identify strengths and planning for learning pathways. Now it's your turn. Take a moment to reflect on the following questions, focusing on how math small groups will benefit the teaching and learning in your classroom.

Learning Intention

After reading this chapter, you will understand how to target the math, identify strengths, and plan pathways for content related to Base-Ten Addition and Subtraction.

Success Criteria

You will be able to use the math content trajectories for Base-Ten Addition and Subtraction, in addition to your State Standards Framework or the *Math Small Group* Standards Trajectory Document, to help you identify the just-right starting place for your students.

The *Math Small Group* Standards Trajectory Document offers a map that shows how all the standards for each domain interrelate. To download this tool, visit resources. corwin.com/mathsmallgroups.

- What ideas did you glean from this chapter that will help you engage in the three steps of the Math Small Group Framework?
- What did you learn about the pathway of Base-Ten Addition and Subtraction across grade levels? How will this help you as you work with your students in the math small group setting?

CHAPTER 9

BASE-TEN MULTIPLICATION AND DIVISION

> ## Learning Intention
>
> After reading this chapter, you will understand how to target the math, identify strengths, and plan pathways for content related to Base-Ten Multiplication and Division.
>
> ## Success Criteria
>
> You will be able to use the math content trajectories for Base-Ten Multiplication and Division, in addition to your State Standards Framework or the *Math Small Group* Standards Trajectory Document, to help you identify the just-right starting place for your students.

CHAPTER INTRODUCTION

Although multiplication and division are typically formally introduced at the end of second grade and the beginning of third grade, multiplication foundations begin as early as kindergarten. The major content in kindergarten and/or first grade includes concepts such as skip counting, doubles, and repeated addition. These skills can be used to begin the formal study of multiplication in Grades 3–5. That said, it is very important not to teach children at the beginning stages that multiplication and repeated addition are the same thing. They are not. Repeated addition is related to the equal groups interpretation of multiplication, but multiplication has a much broader scope.

Regardless of the number sets you are focusing on as you teach multiplication and division (single-digit math facts, multiples of 10 times single-digit numbers, or multidigit numbers), three of the five major interpretations of multiplication should take center stage (see Figure 9.1).

- **Equal Groups Interpretation:** Students use multiple equal groups to represent multiplication or division. For example, they might represent 3 × 4 by sketching 3 circles with 4 stars in each circle.
- **Area/Array Interpretation:** Students use the principle of area, or equal-length rows and columns, to represent multiplication or division. For example, they might use unit squares to show 3 rows of 4 squares for a total of 12 unit squares.

▶ **Multiplicative Comparison:** Students compare two lengths or quantities using multiplication as the comparison. For example, they might use Cuisenaire® rods to show that a brown rod is four times as long as a red rod.

▶ **Rates:** This representation is not covered in Grades K–5 standards.

▶ **Cartesian Products:** This representation is not covered in Grades K–5 standards.

Figure 9.1 • *Five Major Interpretations of Multiplication*

❖ "Groups of"
❖ Rectangular Array/Area
❖ Multiplicative Comparison
❖ Rates
❖ Combinations (fundamental counting principle)

This chapter focuses on the equal groups, area/array, and multiplicative comparison interpretations of multiplication and related division concepts.

BASE-TEN MULTIPLICATION AND DIVISION: AN OVERVIEW

Although most State Standards Frameworks chunk multiplication and division together to a certain degree, they are not as tightly aligned in standards documents as addition and subtraction. Therefore, they appear here as two separate trajectories. That said, they are very much related and should not be taught as completely separate entities. Be sure to help students see the relationship between multiplication and division on an ongoing basis.

The work of multiplication and division begins in grade levels prior to their formal introduction. Young learners focus on skip counting and repeated addition as part of their numeracy work, and these are predecessors to the formalized work in these trajectories. Therefore, you will want to lean into students' prior knowledge of these foundational skills in order to understand what they have become proficient in or where they have unfinished learning.

Typically, beginning around third grade, students begin this work by engaging with the equal groups interpretation of multiplication and division. Be careful not to inadvertently convey that multiplication is the same thing as repeated addition. Although repeated addition relates to the equal groups interpretation, it is not definitive of multiplication as a whole. This is an important idea that will follow students into future grades as they learn, for example, about multiplication as comparison, where they learn that multiplication can be interpreted in different ways. Depending on your grade level, be sure to emphasize the three primary interpretations of multiplication appropriate for Grades 3–5: equal groups, area/array, and multiplicative comparison.

> Depending on your grade level, be sure to emphasize the three primary interpretations of multiplication appropriate for Grades 3–5: equal groups, rectangular area/array, and multiplicative comparison.

As with addition and subtraction, there are several strategies students can lean into when exploring the concept of multiplying and dividing within 100, as seen in Figure 9.2.

Figure 9.2 • *Conceptual Multiplication and Division Strategies*

> ➢ Foundation Facts (×1, ×2, ×5, ×10)
> ➢ Doubling
> ➢ Add-a-Group
> ➢ Subtract-a-Group
> ➢ Squares and Near-Squares
> ➢ Think Multiplication (to divide)

As your students move toward the right of the trajectories, they go through a variety of experiences with multidigit multiplication and division. During these phases, students generalize their foundational understandings as the number sets get increasingly complex. It's important to note that with each level of complexity, students should be developing conceptual understanding first, prior to engaging with standard algorithms (see Figure 9.3).

Figure 9.3 • *Common Conceptual Multiplication and Division Strategies*

> ✓ Break Apart to Multiply
> ✓ Halve and Double
> ✓ Compensation
> ✓ Partial Products
> ✓ Think Multiplication
> ✓ Partial Quotients

In Chapter 4, we discussed the Math Small Group Framework. The content in the rest of this chapter will follow the structure of the framework, pictured again in Figure 9.4.

Figure 9.4 • *Teacher-Facilitated Math Small Group Framework*

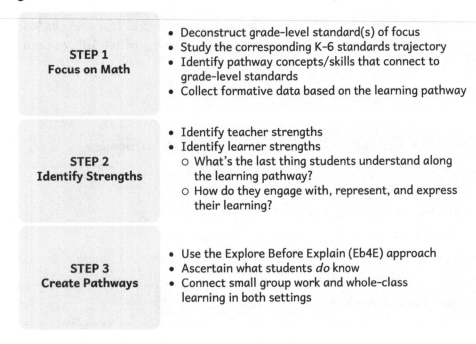

FOCUS ON MATH: MATH CONTENT TRAJECTORIES
FOR BASE-TEN MULTIPLICATION AND DIVISION

For this first step, Focus on Math, you will want to go through four processes to ensure you identify the necessary content for your students. Base-Ten Multiplication and Division spans Grades 3–5 and includes both whole numbers and decimal fractions.

The four processes to engage in as you Focus on Math are as follows:

1. Identify and deconstruct the grade-level standard(s) relevant to Base-Ten Multiplication and Division.

2. Study the Base-Ten Multiplication and Division trajectories in this chapter (see Figure 9.5) as well as in the *Math Small Group Standards Trajectory Document*. You will want to look in domains where multiplication and division unexpectedly appear, such as in the measurement, data, and geometry domains.

3. Identify the multigrade-level pathway concepts and skills that connect to on-grade-level standards for Base-Ten Multiplication and Division. This may include standards from previous grade levels as well as standards for future grade levels. Use whichever standards you need based on the structure (heterogeneous, Guided Math, etc.) and goals for your math small groups.

4. Collect formative data based on the Base-Ten Multiplication and Division standards. Your formative data may include daily entrance or exit tickets, weekly common formative assessments, classroom observational data, or any other data you collect on a regular basis.

Figure 9.5 • *Trajectories for Base-Ten Multiplication and Division*

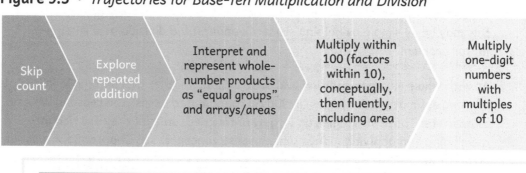

Algebraic Thinking and Overarching Structures

These standards trajectories include several overarching themes as well. They don't generally fall in a specific place along the trajectories. Rather, they appear in several places along the learning continuum, both within and across grade levels. Often, these standards can be used to connect big ideas across domains and grades because they appear so frequently.

Patterns and Generalizations

Although included on the trajectories, one extremely important idea that stretches across grade levels and topics is that of multiplication and division as inverse operations—one "undoes" the other. In early grades, this may be as simple as helping students understand division as a missing-factor problem.

As with whole-number addition and subtraction, another overarching idea is that of using estimation strategies, including rounding, to assess the reasonableness of answers. These strategies go largely untouched, and yet they are rich in developing and applying many number sense concepts. See Chapter 8 for a list of strategies.

Place Value

Place value understanding plays a central role with multidigit arithmetic. Encourage students to use place-value-based strategies and representations such as the area model, composing and decomposing, chunking, and estimating. Regrouping (grouping and ungrouping) plays an especially important role with multiplication and division. You will want to pay close attention to fully develop the place-value-based notions when bundling groups of 10 while multiplying and unbundling groups of 10 while dividing.

Properties

Be sure to continue working with the properties of operations, always embedding them into the way you talk about operations. With multiplication, you will introduce and apply the commutative, associative, identity, zero, and distributive properties of multiplication over addition. Use these properties regularly, paying particular attention to strategies using the distributive property to enhance understanding of the area model early in the multiplication trajectory (see Object 9.1). As with the addition properties, be sure students understand that these properties belong to multiplication and not to division.

Object 9.1 · *Distributive Property for 3 × 8*

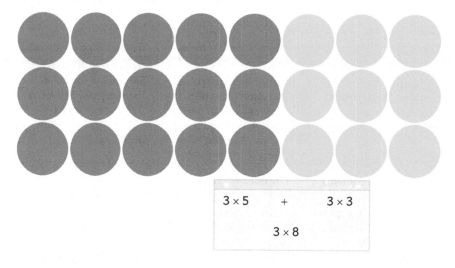

Strategies and Representations

These have been pretty well exhausted in our discussion already. That said, one last and important notion centers on word problems. As with addition and subtraction, be sure to include a variety of word problem situations for each new number set. Generally, students should engage in word problem situations that include equal groups, arrays/area, contexts with measurement units, and comparison (see Figure 9.6). And they should regularly solve problems where the missing number is not always the answer; rather, the missing number should appear in different places within the word problems. And finally, when writing an equation to represent the word problem situation, students should use a symbol to represent the missing number. Many State Standards Frameworks expect that beginning somewhere around third grade, this symbol will be a letter.

> **Fun fact:** When using letters as variables, we conventionally use lowercase letters for algebra (including arithmetic) and uppercase letters for geometry.

With comparison word problem situations, Cuisenaire® rods, linking cubes, place value blocks, and sketched bar models provide an especially good way to demonstrate "times as many."

> Learn more about word problem types from the *Mathematize It!* book series from Corwin.

Figure 9.6 • *Word Problem Types for Multiplication and Division Situations*

Equal Groups of Objects	**(Product Unknown)** Nancy has 5 boxes of cookies. There are 8 cookies in each box. How many cookies does she have in all?	**(Number of Groups Unknown)** Nancy has 40 cookies. She wants to put 5 cookies in each bag. How many bags of cookies will she have when she is finished?	**(Group Size Unknown)** Nancy has 40 cookies. She wants to share them equally between 5 kids. How many cookies will each kid get?
Arrays/Area	**(Product Unknown)** There are 5 rows of cookies with 8 cookies in each row. How many cookies are there in all?	**(One Dimension Unknown)** If 40 cookies are arranged in 5 rows, how many cookies are in each row?	**(Both Dimensions Unknown)** There are 40 cookies arranged in a rectangular array. How many cookies might be in each row and column?
Multiplicative Comparison	**(Resulting Value Unknown)** A small box holds 8 cookies. A large box holds 5 times as many cookies as a small box. How many cookies fit in the large box?	**(Scale Factor Unknown)** A large box holds 40 cookies and a small box holds 8 cookies. How many times more cookies does a large box hold than a small box?	**(Original Value Unknown)** A large cookie box holds 40 cookies, and that is 8 times as many as a small box. How many cookies does a small box hold?

MATH TOOLS TO SUPPORT THESE TRAJECTORIES

When preparing for your math small groups, you may be planning for math concepts and skills that are not necessarily at your grade level. The suggestions in this section are intended to help you think through the materials you may need, especially for facilitating conceptual development.

As you gather materials, be mindful that you include a wide variety to encourage students to translate within and across the different categories of representations: concrete (manipulatives and objects), visual, symbolic, verbal, and contextual (Lesh et al., 1987). You should encourage students to represent their thinking in ways that make sense to them, giving them choice as much as possible. In addition, ask students to work side by side with different representations and then compare and contrast what they see. This will help students make sense of their thinking as well as develop new ways of thinking about the concepts and skills at hand.

See Chapter 2 for more information about the Lesh Translation Model of Representations.

Concrete Representations

Counters: When beginning the study of multiplication, provide a variety of counters (beans, cereal pieces, plastic discs, or any variety of small items) for students to use. Counters are especially useful for exploring the equal groups interpretation of multiplication and division within 100.

Linking Cubes: Like counters, linking cubes offer a great option for students to explore the equal groups interpretation of multiplication and division. Linking cubes have the added benefit of being able to snap together into equal groups, facilitating a great way for students to visualize multiplication and division within 100 (see Object 9.2).

Object 9.2 · *Linking Cubes Representing Equal Groups Multiplication*

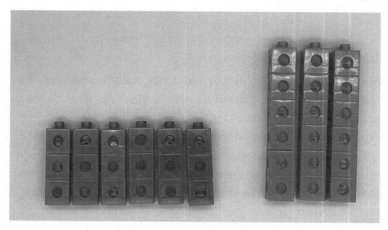

Unit Tiles: These one-inch squares provide a fantastic way for students to explore the array/area model for multiplication. Although any counters can be put into arrays, square tiles have the added attribute of fitting together with no gaps and no overlaps. In this way, you can directly connect the concept of area to multiplication (see Object 9.3).

Object 9.3 · *Unit Tiles Representing the Area Model of Multiplication*

Cuisenaire® Rods: This unique tool provides a great way for students to investigate the comparison interpretation of multiplication, an important building block for ratios and proportions and linear equations later down the road (see Object 9.4).

Object 9.4 · *Cuisenaire® Rods Representing Multiplicative Comparison*

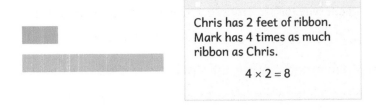

Chris has 2 feet of ribbon.
Mark has 4 times as much ribbon as Chris.

$$4 \times 2 = 8$$

Base-Ten Manipulatives: Base-ten blocks and other pregrouped base-ten manipulatives like KP® Ten-Frame Tiles work well as students explore the concepts of multidigit multiplication and division (see Objects 9.5 and 9.6). Note that there are two interpretations of division to attend to: partitive and quotative. When students represent partitive division (a.k.a. "fair-share" division), they use the divisor to determine the number of groups and then divide the manipulatives equally into those groups. On the other hand, when they represent quotative division (a.k.a. "measurement" division), they use the divisor to determine the group size, and then divide the objects into divisor-sized groups to determine how many groups they can make.

Object 9.5 · *Base-Ten Blocks Representing the Area Model of Multiplication*

12×24

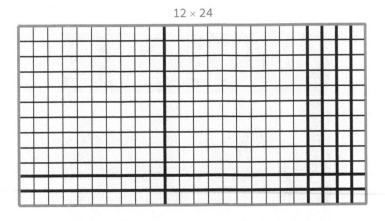

Object 9.6 · *KP® Ten-Frame Tiles Representing the Quotative Division*

$$95 \div 4 = 23 \, R3$$

20 × 4 = 80

3 × 4 = 12

R3

Visual Representations

Sketching: Ask students to sketch their representations as much as possible. This may include any of the previously mentioned interpretations: equal groups, arrays/area models, and comparison models. When sketching multiplication and division models, be sure to encourage your students to note the units as a support as they interpret and solve the problems.

Open Arrays: This method for helping students visualize partial products and quotients is specifically connected to the area/array model (see Object 9.7).

Object 9.7 · *Area/Array Model With Partial Products*

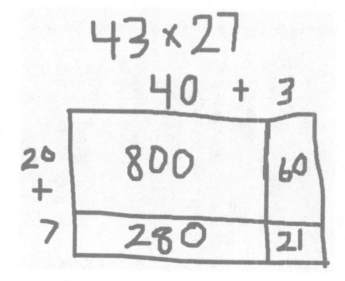

$$43 \times 27$$

40 + 3

	40	3
20	800	60
7	280	21

Hundreds Charts: Hundreds charts also make terrific work mats for students to identify patterns when working with multiplication within 100 (see Object 9.8).

Object 9.8 · *Hundreds Chart Patterns*

1	2	3	4	5	6	7	8	9	10
11	12	13	14	15	16	17	18	19	20
21	22	23	24	25	26	27	28	29	30
31	32	33	34	35	36	37	38	39	40
41	42	43	44	45	46	47	48	49	50
51	52	53	54	55	56	57	58	59	60
61	62	63	64	65	66	67	68	69	70
71	72	73	74	75	76	77	78	79	80
81	82	83	84	85	86	87	88	89	90
91	92	93	94	95	96	97	98	99	100

Symbolic Representations

Conceptual Multiplication and Division: When students record their work, encourage them to use symbols to represent various aspects of their conceptual drawings. For example, students should label the equal groups sketches with equations as well as record the expressions/equations associated with the partial products in an open-array diagram (see Object 9.9).

Object 9.9 · *Partial Products With KP® Ten-Frame Tiles and Symbols*

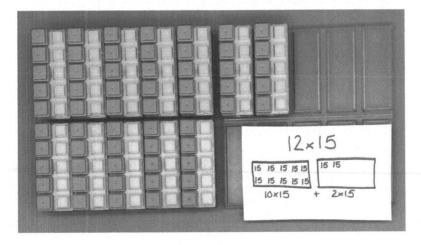

Standard Algorithms: Quite often, we introduce standard algorithms far too soon in the learning sequence. Many State Standards Frameworks expect that students do not use standard algorithms for multiplication until fifth grade and for division until sixth grade. Until then, students should use conceptual strategies based on place value, properties of operations, and the relationship between multiplication and division. Students may still use symbolic representations to represent their thinking, but standard algorithm work can wait until later so students can fully develop understanding beforehand.

Verbal Representations

Sentence Starters: Think ahead about what kinds of prompts you might provide to students to get them talking about whole-number multiplication and division. Create an anchor chart or a set of cards on a binder ring that provide sentence starters for your students. Here are a few to get you started:

- When I multiply ___ and ___, the product is going to be about ___. I know this because . . .

- When I divide ___ and ___, the quotient is going to be about ___. I know this because . . .

- Multiplication and division are similar because . . .

- Multiplication and division are different because . . .

Verbal Explanations: During math small groups, ask students to explain and describe their thinking. This might include asking them to whisper-talk to themselves as they describe the steps they're using to multiply and divide. Sometimes, saying things out loud helps us make sense of our own work or realize where we've made an error in our thinking or calculations.

Furthermore, ask your students to read multiplication and division equations with meaning. For example, the expression $24 \div 8$ might be read as either "24 shared into groups-of-8" or "24 shared into 8 equal-sized groups." This provides a connection for understanding when students encounter more complex fraction and decimal-fraction division. In this instance, the expression $5 \div 0.4$ might be read as "5 partitioned into groups-of-0.4," or $1.3 \div 3$ could be read as "1.3 partitioned into 3 equal-sized groups."

Written Explanations: Ask students to write about their thinking at different times. Here are two prompts you might want to consider: "What are the steps you used to find your solution?" and "How do you know your solution is correct? Prove it."

Contextual Representations

Teacher-Created Context Problems: Whenever possible, provide context to help students engage with the multiplication and division operations. Use people, places, and situations that are of high interest to your students, specifically, or to their age group, generally.

Student-Created Context Problems: Ask students to create their own contexts for the multiplication and division problems. You can simply provide the expression or equation, and students compose the word problem. This can bring a bit of playfulness into your small groups, allowing students to make their own connections between math and the real world. It also provides you with insights into their understanding of the behaviors of multiplication and division. This technique can also uncover the flexibility a student is developing with regard to the concept of multiplication or division.

Recording Materials

Provide a variety of recording materials for students to use, including blank paper, dry-erase boards, markers, colored pencils, pencils, and erasers.

IDENTIFY STRENGTHS: SAMPLE PROMPTS FOR DETECTING LEARNERS' CONTENT STRENGTHS

Identifying strengths regarding Base-Ten Multiplication and Division includes finding out what students already know about multiplicative thinking.

Keep in mind that identifying strengths includes a focus on both you and your students.

1. **Identify teacher strengths:** What do you know about the five interpretations of multiplication, three of which are used in Grades K–5? How will you tap into the multiplication foundations laid in Grades K–2 with topics such as skip counting, doubles, and repeated addition? How do you talk about multiplication and division conceptually without using a formal algorithm? How do you use multiplication- and division-specific representations to show these operations without using a formal algorithm? How do you talk about the properties of multiplication conceptually?

2. **Identify learner strengths:** Use the formative data you've collected as well as the sample prompts that follow to determine learner strengths. What's the last thing your students *do* understand along the learning pathway? How do they engage with, represent, and express their learning?

The goal of using these prompts is to help you identify the last thing the student knows about this particular concept or skill. This will be the starting place for your math small group work, building on successes and connecting to new learning. This provides valuable information as you plan for your teacher-facilitated math small groups.

Multiplication and Division as Inverse Operations: Show students a full multiplication equation such as $3 \times 5 = 15$ or $12 \times 15 = 180$. Then ask them to name a related division problem and explain why the two are related. For example, they might say, "$3 \times 5 = 15$ is related to $15 \div 5 = 3$ because when you're multiplying, you're putting together 3 groups of 5, which is the same value as 15.

And when you're dividing, you're taking apart 15 into 3 groups of 5 (or 5 groups of 3)." Record your students' successes and growth points.

Using Models for Multiplication or Division Facts: Place a set of 24 unit squares in front of each student. Ask them to use the tiles to show 3 × 6 or 18 ÷ 3. Then ask them to describe how their representation shows multiplication. For example, they might say, "I put the squares into three rows of 6, and three 6s are the same value as 18." Note what interpretation they use (e.g., equal groups or area/array). Record your students' successes and growth points.

Using Models for the Distributive Property of Multiplication: Place 18 unit squares in front of each student. Ask them to build a 3 × 6 rectangle. Then ask them how the rectangle can be described using multiplication. Finally, ask them if there is a way to break apart the rectangle into two parts that would make finding the total easier and to describe what they did. If successful, note how they broke apart the array (e.g., two 3 × 3 arrays to show two groups of 9, which is still 18; or one 3 × 5 array and one 3 × 1 array to show 15 and 3, which is still 18). Record your students' successes and growth points.

Using Models for Multidigit Multiplication: Ask students to sketch a model that shows 12 × 15 = 180. What interpretation do they use (e.g., equal groups or area/array)? What representations do they use (e.g., dots, chart, number line, symbols; see Object 9.10)? How do they describe the relationship between their sketch and multiplication? Record your students' successes and growth points.

Object 9.10 · *Different Models for Multidigit Multiplication*

CREATE PATHWAYS: SAMPLE TEACHER-FACILITATED SMALL GROUP LESSONS

When creating learning pathways, consider what you've learned about student strengths as starting points to build upon.

The three components for Creating Pathways are as follows:

- ▸ Use the Explore Before Explain (Eb4E) Lesson Planning Template to plan your lesson.
- ▸ Consider what you learned about your students' strengths—what do they already know about Base-Ten Multiplication and Division?
- ▸ Connect Base-Ten Multiplication and Division concepts between your math small group work and whole-class learning. Use Base-Ten Multiplication and Division routines in both settings to help students make connections.

> To download the Eb4E Lesson Planning Template, visit resources.corwin.com/mathsmallgroups.

The following selected sample lessons provide examples for how you might design a math small group lesson, attending to each area of the framework. Note that these examples can be easily adapted for students working with all number sets.

Becoming Undone

Focus on Math: In this activity, students connect multiplication and division as inverse operations to your current grade-level content.

Identify Student Strengths: Prior to this activity, identify students' strengths and growth points by using the "Multiplication and Division as Inverse Operations" prompt (p. 170) or something similar. Use student strengths to connect to new learning.

Materials:

- Unit squares
- Dry-erase boards and markers (or paper and pencils)

Create Pathways:

Launch

1. Ask students to make rectangles with 12 unit squares. Challenge them as a group to make as many different rectangles as possible.

2. Point to just one, perhaps a 3 × 4 array, and ask students to describe it using multiplication. Then ask them to describe it using division.

3. Use prompting and probing questions as needed to help students distinguish between putting together 3 rows of 4 unit squares to make 12 (multiplication) or starting with 12 and splitting it into 3 rows with 4 unit squares in each row (division). For example:

   ▸ Tell me about this 3 × 4 array. How many rows? How many columns?

   ▸ How might you use this array to describe multiplication?

   ▸ How might you use this array to describe division?

Explore

1. Have students work with partners to repeat this process using 16 unit squares.

2. Have students use objects, sketches, equations, and words to show how each rectangle can show both multiplication and division. As you do this, you might find it useful to discuss the notion that a square *is* a rectangle. Many students continue to struggle with this geometric concept, and this is a good time to review it.

Discuss

1. Use prompting and probing questions to support students as they explain how their rectangles can be described using both multiplication and division.

   - How can you use multiplication to describe this rectangle?
   - How can you use division to describe this rectangle?
   - What is similar about the multiplication and division equations you used to name this rectangle?
   - Why can the same rectangle be used to show both multiplication and division?

2. If students have difficulty talking about the relationship between multiplication and division, model the language for them and ask them to try to explain with another rectangle. Encourage them to "ask a friend" if they get stuck.

Wrap Up

1. **Check for Understanding:** Show students a 2 × 4 rectangle. Ask them to write a multiplication equation and a division equation to describe the rectangle. Then ask them to write one or two sentences explaining why the rectangle can represent both multiplication and division.

2. **Connect to Grade-Level Content:** Explicitly connect the relationship between multiplication and division to your current grade-level content, during both small group and whole-class time.

ACTIVITY 9.2

Breaking Up Is (Not) So Hard to Do

Focus on Math: In this activity, students connect the distributive property for multiplication facts to your current grade-level content.

Identify Student Strengths: Prior to this activity, identify students' strengths and growth points by using the "Using Models for the Distributive Property of Multiplication" prompt (p. 171) or something similar. Use student strengths to connect to new learning.

Materials:

- Unit squares
- Dry-erase boards and markers or paper and pencils

Create Pathways:

Launch

1. Using the unit squares, place a 2 × 8 array in front of the students.
2. Ask students to describe the array using multiplication.
3. Ask students how they might break it into two rectangles that are easier to multiply.
4. Ask prompting and probing questions to help students see the following possibilities:
   - Two 2 × 4 arrays to show 8 and 8
   - One 2 × 5 array and one 2 × 3 array to show 10 and 6
   - Two 1 × 8 arrays to show 8 and 8
5. Ask students to describe and demonstrate the idea that no matter how they break it apart, it still represents a total of 16.

Explore

1. Divide students into pairs.
2. Have pairs work with unit squares to show different ways to break apart the following expressions: 2 × 6, 3 × 6, 4 × 6, 3 × 7, and 4 × 7. Have them record their work using sketches and numbers. Ask prompting and proving questions such as the following:
   - Can we break apart a different factor? What might that look like?
   - Are there facts related to the factors that you already know? How can you use these known facts?

3. Continue with more as time allows. For each rectangle built, ask students to break it apart into smaller rectangles that are easier to multiply. Have them record their work using sketches and numbers.

Discuss

1. Ask students to choose one rectangle that everyone worked on.

2. Use prompting and probing questions to help students describe different ways to break apart the rectangle to make the multiplication easier.

   - Describe one of the arrays that you made. How many rows? How many columns?

   - Which side on the array did you want to break apart?

   - How did you separate the array to show two easier multiplications?

3. Using their work as a reference, have students sketch the different configurations and label them with expressions.

4. Introduce the phrase *distributive property* and show how students were using the distributive property when they split apart the rectangles.

Wrap Up

1. **Check for Understanding:** Display a 2 × 7 array. Ask students to use the distributive property to show a simpler way to multiply.

2. **Connect to Grade-Level Content:** Explicitly connect the distributive property for multiplication facts to your current grade-level content, during both small group and whole-class time.

Multiplication Always Makes a Rectangle

Focus on Math: In this activity, students connect using the area model for multidigit multiplication to your current grade-level content.

Identify Student Strengths: Prior to this activity, identify students' strengths and growth points by using the "Using the Models for Multidigit Multiplication" prompt (p. 171) or something similar. Use student strengths to connect to new learning.

Materials:

- Unit squares
- Base-ten blocks
- Dry-erase boards and markers or paper and pencils

Create Pathways:

Launch

1. Display a 3 × 4 unit square rectangle.
2. Ask students what they know about the relationship between rectangles and multiplication. Sample response: "If I show multiplication with a rectangle with same-sized squares, then there will be equal-length rows that make a rectangle. For example, if I show 3 × 4 with same-sized unit squares, then there are 3 rows with 4 squares in each row."
3. Display a 13 × 14 array using base-ten blocks.
4. Ask students to describe why/how this rectangle also represents multiplication.

Explore

1. Divide students into pairs.
2. Have pairs represent the 13 × 14 array using sketches and numbers.
3. Support students as they sketch the base-ten blocks. Help them see the four partial products that emerge as they build the array.
4. Ask students to describe contexts in which the area model might be useful. Examples include laying carpet squares, cutting a sheet cake into square-shaped pieces, placing chairs for the audience to watch a play, and so on.

Discuss

1. Ask students to describe the arrays they sketched.

2. Introduce the idea of a short-cut sketch with an open array (illustrated in Object 9.11).

Object 9.11 · *Open-Array Sketch*

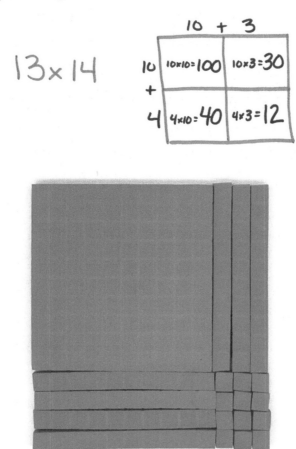

3. Talk about how the open array relates to the base-ten block model.

Wrap Up

1. **Check for Understanding:** Have students record a written explanation for how the 13 × 14 array, built with base-ten blocks, has four partial products and why this is the same total number of squares as the entire 13 × 14 array.

2. **Connect to Grade-Level Content:** Explicitly connect using the area model for multidigit multiplication to your current grade-level content, during both small group and whole-class time.

YOUR TURN

Throughout this chapter, you had the chance to view math small groups through the lens of the Math Small Group Framework. You focused on the math in the Base-Ten Multiplication and Division standards, looking at ways to identify strengths and planning for learning pathways. Now it's your turn. Take a moment to reflect on the following questions, focusing on how math small groups will benefit the teaching and learning in your classroom.

Learning Intention

After reading this chapter, you will understand how to target the math, identify strengths, and plan pathways for content related to Base-Ten Multiplication and Division.

Success Criteria

You will be able to use the math content trajectories for Base-Ten Multiplication and Division, in addition to your State Standards Framework or the *Math Small Group* Standards Trajectory Document, to help you identify the just-right starting place for your students.

The *Math Small Group* Standards Trajectory Document offers a map that shows how all the standards for each domain interrelate. To download this tool, visit resources.corwin.com/mathsmallgroups.

- What ideas did you glean from this chapter that will help you engage in the three steps of the Math Small Group Framework?

- What did you learn about the pathway of Base-Ten Multiplication and Division across grade levels? How will this help you as you work with your students in the math small group setting?

CHAPTER 10

FRACTION FOUNDATIONS

> ## Learning Intention
>
> After reading this chapter, you will understand how to target the math, identify strengths, and plan pathways for content related to Fraction Foundations.
>
> ## Success Criteria
>
> You will be able to use the math content trajectory for Fraction Foundations, in addition to your State Standards Framework or the *Math Small Group* Standards Trajectory Document, to help you identify the just-right starting place for your students.

CHAPTER INTRODUCTION

Fraction Foundations begin in Grades K–2, typically located alongside the geometry standards, as students partition circles and rectangles into fractional pieces. This lays the foundation for Grades 3–5, where students begin their formal work with fractions. It is during these years that unit fractions, fractions on number lines, equivalent fractions, and fraction operations are introduced. In most State Standards Frameworks, fraction work remains conceptual until the end of the fractions trajectory, typically in fifth and/or sixth grade.

In this chapter, you will explore the many ideas introduced across the grade levels in preparation for supporting your teacher-facilitated math small groups with fraction foundations. Quite often, you'll want to temporarily dip into content covered in previous grade levels to ensure a cohesive understanding of the many foundational ideas. Of course, as you venture into the previous years' content, you'll want to quickly connect it to your current-level content.

FRACTION FOUNDATIONS: AN OVERVIEW

Work with fractions typically begins in kindergarten or first grade through partitioning geometric shapes into fractional pieces. As you plan fractions pathways for your math small groups, be sure to look at the geometry domain to find hiding fractions standards. In these early years, students focus on partitioning circles and rectangles (including square-shaped rectangles) into halves, thirds, and fourths. They explore ideas such as the following:

- Fractional pieces of the same whole must be the same size but not necessarily the same shape.

- The name of the fraction tells you how many parts will cover the whole. Students use two halves to cover one whole, three thirds to cover one whole, and four fourths to cover one whole. These should be referred to as "one-half-sized pieces, one-third-sized pieces, and one-fourth-sized pieces."

- A shape can be partitioned into fractional parts in more than one way.

Although young students do not necessarily use fraction notation prior to third grade, they become fluent with the language of fractions: halves, half of, fourths, quarters, and so on.

Typically in third grade, students begin their formal work with fractions, including notation. A major part of the work centers on deeply understanding unit fractions and their applications to composing/decomposing, equivalence, addition, subtraction, multiplication, division, and so much more. Third graders use unit fractions understanding to count by fractions, compose and decompose both proper and improper fractions, and compare fractions.

From the beginning, students should focus on the three major types of fractional models: area models, linear models, and set models (see Figure 10.1). They should also spend a significant amount of time investigating the relationship between the numerator (how many pieces) and the denominator (what kind of fraction) while creating models that fit into all three categories.

Figure 10.1 · *Three Categories of Fraction Models*

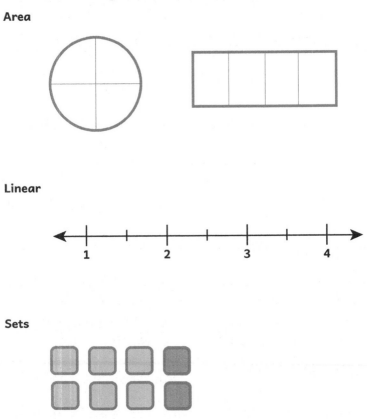

In addition to working with unit fractions, most State Standards Frameworks begin the formal work with equivalence in third grade using conceptual models, completing that sequence around fifth grade, where students are expected to apply their understanding of equivalent fractions for the purpose of adding and subtracting fractions. During the time in between, students are using unit fractions as the primary way to build conceptual understanding with fraction addition, subtraction, and multiplication with both proper fractions and mixed numbers.

As for comparing fractions, students should use mental strategies such as comparing fractions with like numerators and like denominators, comparing fractions to benchmark fractions, and comparing fractions to the nearest whole number (see Figure 10.2). These four strategies should be exhausted prior to trying the equivalent fractions method. This use of fraction sense is powerful in helping students grapple with the foundational underpinnings.

Figure 10.2 • *Methods for Comparing Fractions*

- Same denominators – Different number of same-sized pieces
- Same numerators – Same number of different-sized pieces
- Compare to a benchmark (e.g., $\frac{1}{2}$, 1 whole)
- Size of "missing piece" (e.g., $\frac{7}{8}$ vs. $\frac{5}{6}$ – the missing sixth is larger than the missing seventh, so $\frac{7}{8}$ is greater than $\frac{5}{6}$)

The final component of this standards trajectory centers on interpreting fractions as division of the numerator by the denominator. You might want to make this connection all the way back in third grade when division is first introduced. Students would benefit from knowing that 12 ÷ 3 can also be written as $\frac{12}{3}$. It's no accident that the ÷ symbol actually looks like a fraction! If you decide to share this convention with young students, you might ask students to review and explore the notion that equal groups with fractions is the same as equal groups with division.

In Chapter 4, we discussed the Math Small Group Framework. The content in the rest of this chapter will follow the structure of the framework, pictured again in Figure 10.3.

Figure 10.3 · *Teacher-Facilitated Math Small Group Framework*

STEP 1 **Focus on Math**	• Deconstruct grade-level standard(s) of focus • Study the corresponding K-6 standards trajectory • Identify pathway concepts/skills that connect to grade-level standards • Collect formative data based on the learning pathway

STEP 2
Identify Strengths
	• Identify teacher strengths
	• Identify learner strengths
	  o What's the last thing students understand along the learning pathway?
	  o How do they engage with, represent, and express their learning?

STEP 3 **Create Pathways**	• Use the Explore Before Explain (Eb4E) approach • Ascertain what students *do* know • Connect small group work and whole-class learning in both settings

FOCUS ON MATH: MATH CONTENT TRAJECTORY FOR FRACTION FOUNDATIONS

For this first step, Focus on Math, you will want to go through four processes to ensure you identify the necessary content for your students. Fraction Foundations spans Grades K–5 and includes both whole numbers and decimal fractions.

The four processes to engage in as you Focus on Math are as follows:

1. Identify and deconstruct the grade-level standard(s) relevant to Fraction Foundations.

2. Study the Fraction Foundations trajectory in Figure 10.4 as well as in the *Math Small Group* Standards Trajectory Document.

3. Identify the multigrade-level pathway concepts and skills that connect to on-grade-level standards for Fraction Foundations. This may include standards from previous grade levels as well as standards for future grade levels. Use whichever standards you need based on the structure (heterogeneous, Guided Math, etc.) and goals for your math small groups.

Figure 10.4 • *Trajectory for Fraction Foundations.*

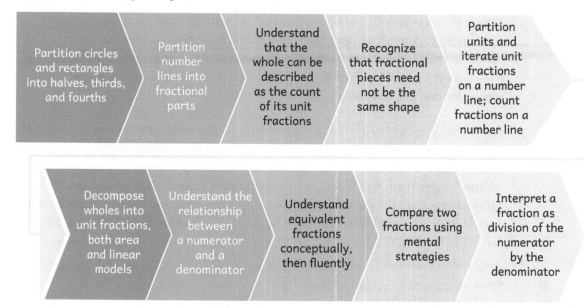

Collect formative data based on the Fraction Foundations standards. Your formative data may include daily entrance or exit tickets, weekly common formative assessments, classroom observational data, or any other data you collect on a regular basis.

Algebraic Thinking and Overarching Structures

This standards trajectory includes several overarching themes as well. They don't generally fall in a specific place along the trajectory; rather, they appear in several places along the learning continuum, both within and across grade levels. Often, these standards can be used to connect big ideas across domains and grades because they appear so frequently.

Patterns and Generalizations

The formal study of unit fractions usually appears somewhere around the third-grade standards. Because the application of unit fractions permeates the standards across grade levels, both formally and informally, you will want to capitalize on this powerful tool in your math small groups. Another important generalization to point out centers on the notion that although a fraction is comprised of two numerals, it represents a single number. That number is represented by the relationship between the partitioned whole and its given number of same-sized pieces.

Properties

Although the properties of operations do not tend to make an appearance in the fractions domain of most State Standards Frameworks, you may want to continue reinforcing all of them throughout your fractions work. Commutativity, Associativity, and Distributivity are all still part of the deal—you can still add in any order and get the same sum.

The identity property of multiplication may be the most powerful application of the properties for students as they work with equivalent fractions. In essence, when students are finding equivalent fractions, they are multiplying by a "form of one" to get from one fraction to another (see Object 10.1). Rather than telling them that they are "multiplying the numerator and denominator by the same factor," talk about multiplying by $\frac{2}{2}, \frac{3}{3}, \frac{4}{4}, \frac{10}{10}$, and so on— all different ways for renaming "1."

Strategies and Representations

We have already covered most of the overarching strategies and representations that are most valuable for students when developing "fraction sense," such as the three basic fraction models, the application of unit fractions as strategies for fraction operations, and the use of reasoning to compare fractions. You may also want to regularly reference the use of benchmark fractions and number sense to estimate mentally and assess the reasonableness of answers, mirroring the estimation work done with whole numbers.

Object 10.1 • *Equivalent Fractions Using the Identity Property of Multiplication*

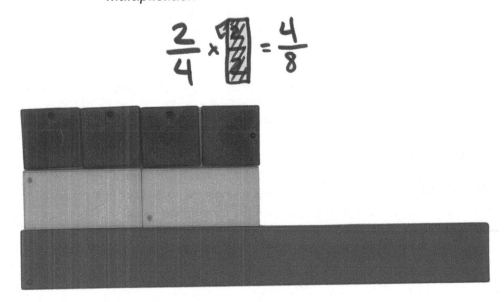

Remember that the three basic fraction models (area models, linear models such as number lines, and sets of objects) present very distinct views for representing fractions. Be sure to include all three of them when working with fractions. Your students may find it helpful to translate from one model to another as a strategy to rewrite fractions in different forms. This is especially true for greater-than-1 fractions that can be written as improper fractions, mixed numbers, and decimal fractions.

MATH TOOLS TO SUPPORT THIS TRAJECTORY

When preparing for your math small groups, you may be planning for math concepts and skills that are not necessarily at your grade level. The suggestions in this section are intended to help you think through the materials you may need, especially for facilitating conceptual development.

As you gather materials, be mindful that you include a wide variety to encourage students to translate within and across the different categories of representations: concrete (manipulatives and objects), visual, symbolic, verbal, and contextual (Lesh et al., 1987). You should encourage students to represent their thinking in ways that make sense to them, giving them choice as much as possible. In addition, ask students to work side by side with different representations and then compare and contrast what they see. This will help students make sense of their thinking as well as develop new ways of thinking about the concepts and skills at hand.

See Chapter 2 for more information about the Lesh Translation Model of Representations.

Concrete Representations

Providing students with a variety of fraction models helps them generate flexibility with defining the unit, or "whole," in a variety of ways. You can use commercial, virtual, or homemade fraction manipulatives, including fraction circles, squares, tiles/bars, and towers. You can also use Cuisenaire® rods or pattern blocks to explore fractional relationships. Or, you may simply want to use paper shapes, asking your students to cut or fold paper shapes into same-sized fraction pieces (Moore & Rimbey, 2021).

Note that when working with commercial fraction pieces, students will be better off with fraction pieces that have no markings on them. That way, the "whole" can be redefined, depending on the operations and number sets.

Visual Representations

Having students sketch their fraction work will increase the likelihood that it will transfer to long-term memory. Students typically sketch objects similar to the fraction pieces illustrated in Object 10.1. Provide them with plenty of writing materials so they can use color to support their thinking about fractions. Color makes a big difference when your students are trying to represent ideas such as fractional parts of fractional parts.

Symbolic Representations

With most students introduced to fraction notation somewhere around third grade, you'll want to spend significant time helping them connect the fraction symbols to their meaning. Helping students understand the relationship between the numerator, which tells how many pieces, and the denominator, which tells what kind of pieces, will be critical to their future success. Guiding students in their understanding of the identity property as the mechanism for finding equivalent fractions in later grades proves to be another key idea with far-reaching implications.

Verbal Representations

Sentence Starters: Think ahead about what kinds of prompts you might provide to your students to get them talking about fraction concepts. Create an anchor chart or a set of cards on a binder ring that provide sentence starters for students, such as the following:

- A fraction is a number that describes . . .
- The numerator describes . . .
- The denominator describes . . .
- I know this fraction describes more than that fraction because . . .
- I know these two fractions describe the same amount because . . .

Verbal Explanations: When working with fraction concepts, ask students to explain and describe their thinking. This might include asking them to whisper-talk to themselves as they describe the steps they're using to multiply and divide. Sometimes saying things out loud helps us make sense of our own work or realize where we've made an error in our thinking or calculations. Specifically, your students might find it helpful to translate back and forth with word form and symbol form. For example, describing $\frac{3}{4}$ as 3 one-fourth-sized pieces helps remind them what the symbols represent.

Written Explanations: Ask students to write about their thinking at different times. Here are two prompts you might want to consider: "What are the steps you used to find your solution?" and "How do you know your solution is correct? Prove it."

Contextual Representations

Teacher-Created Context Problems: Whenever possible, provide context to help students engage with Fraction Foundations. Use people, places, and situations that are of high interest to your students, specifically, or to their age group, generally.

Student-Created Context Problems: You may also want to ask the students to create their own contexts to demonstrate fraction understanding. You provide the symbolic representations, and students compose the word problem. This can bring a bit of playfulness into your small groups, allowing students to make their own connections between math and the real world. It also provides you with insights into their understanding of the behaviors of fractions.

Recording Materials

Provide a variety of recording materials for students to use, including blank paper, dry-erase boards, markers, colored pencils, pencils, and erasers.

IDENTIFY STRENGTHS: SAMPLE PROMPTS FOR DETECTING LEARNERS' CONTENT STRENGTHS

Identifying strengths regarding Fraction Foundations includes finding out what students already know about multiplicative thinking.

Keep in mind that identifying strengths includes a focus on both you and your students.

1. **Identify teacher strengths:** How do you describe numerators (number of pieces) and denominators (size of pieces) (e.g., "one-fourth-sized pieces")? How do you partition geometric shapes into fractional pieces? How do you talk about Fraction Foundations conceptually without using formal algorithms? How do you talk about and use fraction-specific representations to illustrate Fraction Foundations?

2. **Identify learner strengths:** Use the formative data you've collected as well as the sample prompts that follow to determine learner strengths. What's the last thing students *do* understand along the learning pathway? How do they engage with, represent, and express their learning?

The goal of using these prompts is to help you identify the last thing the student knows about this particular concept or skill. This will be the starting place for your math small group work, building on successes and connecting to new learning. This provides valuable information as you plan for your teacher-facilitated math small groups.

Unit Fractions

Ask each student to draw a rectangle and partition it into fourths. Ask, "What do you call one piece?" Then ask students to write the fraction that represents one piece. Repeat with a rectangle partitioned into thirds and a square partitioned into halves. Record your students' successes and growth points. You can repeat using other fractions.

Comparing Fractions

Write the following fractions on a note card: $\frac{3}{1}$ and $\frac{1}{1}$. Ask each student which fraction represents more and why (sample answer: $\frac{3}{1}$ is more because there are more of the same-sized pieces). Next, show the fractions $\frac{2}{3}$ and $\frac{2}{5}$ and ask which fraction represents more and why (sample answer: $\frac{2}{3}$ because the pieces are bigger). Finally, show the fractions $\frac{5}{8}$ and $\frac{2}{5}$ and ask which fraction represents more and why (sample answer: $\frac{5}{8}$ because it's more than $\frac{1}{2}$ and $\frac{2}{5}$ is less than $\frac{1}{2}$). Record your students' successes and growth points. You can repeat using other fractions.

Equivalent Fractions

Show students two fractions: $\frac{2}{16}$ and $\frac{1}{8}$. Ask students to describe the relationship between these two fractions. (Sample responses: $\frac{2}{16}$ and $\frac{1}{8}$ are equivalent because they name the same amount. Or, $\frac{2}{16}$ is the same amount as $\frac{1}{8}$, only the pieces are smaller and you have more of them.) If students are successful with this prompt, ask them to draw a sketch that demonstrates why these two fractions are equivalent. If they are unsuccessful with this prompt, you draw a sketch of the two fractions and ask again for them to describe the relationship between these two fractions. Record your students' successes and growth points. You can repeat using other fractions.

CREATE PATHWAYS: SAMPLE TEACHER-FACILITATED SMALL GROUP LESSONS

When creating learning pathways, consider what you've learned about student strengths as starting points to build upon.

The three components for Creating Pathways are as follows:

▶ Use the Explore Before Explain (Eb4E) Lesson Planning Template to plan your lesson.

▶ Consider what you learned about your students' strengths—what do they already know about Fraction Foundations?

▶ Connect Fraction Foundations concepts between your math small group work and whole-class learning. Use Fraction Foundations routines in both settings to help students make connections.

> To download the Eb4E Lesson Planning Template, visit resources.corwin.com/mathsmallgroups.

The following selected sample lessons provide examples for how you might design a math small group lesson, attending to each area of the framework. Note that these examples can be easily adapted for students working with all number sets.

ACTIVITY 10.1

Unit Fractions

Focus on Math: In this activity, students connect unit fractions to your current grade-level content.

Identify Student Strengths: Prior to this activity, identify students' strengths and growth points by using the "Unit Fractions" prompt (p. 190) or something similar. Use student strengths to connect to new learning.

Materials:

- Fraction manipulatives with no fractions written on them (circles, squares, bars, pattern blocks, etc.)
- Dry-erase boards and markers or paper and pencils

Create Pathways:

Launch

1. Show students a circle partitioned into thirds, a square partitioned into fourths, and a rectangle partitioned into fifths.
2. Ask students to create a "context" for each picture. For example, we can pretend the circle is a pie cut into thirds, the square is a window divided into four panes, and the rectangle is a piece of craft paper folded into fifths.
3. Use prompting and probing questions to help the students recognize that each piece in those shapes has a unique name. Each piece of the pie is $\frac{1}{3}$ of the whole, each piece of the window is $\frac{1}{4}$ of the whole, and each section of the paper is $\frac{1}{5}$ of the whole.
   - How many same-sized pieces make the circle? What is the name of the fraction that describes each of those pieces?
   - How many same-sized pieces make the square? What is the name of the fraction that describes each of those pieces?
   - How many same-sized pieces make the rectangle? What is the name of the fraction that describes each of those pieces?

Explore

1. Divide students into pairs.
2. Have pairs create their own scenarios using the fraction piece manipulatives, recording them on dry-erase boards or paper. They

should both sketch the "picture" and label each part with its unit fraction.

3. Use prompting and probing questions to facilitate thinking if students get stuck:

   - Which fraction pieces are you going to use?
   - What is the name of the whole?
   - How many same-sized pieces did you partition the whole into?
   - What is the name of the fraction that describes each of those pieces?

Discuss

1. Use prompting and probing questions to help students attach meaning to their drawings:

   - How many pieces is your round pizza cut into (e.g., six pieces)?
   - What do you call the size of those pieces (e.g., sixths)?
   - What is the name of each piece (e.g., one sixth)?
   - How do you write that as a fraction (e.g., $\frac{1}{6}$)?
   - Why?

2. Be sure that by the end, students can communicate that the denominator tells the size of the equal-sized pieces in relation to the whole, the numerator tells how many pieces we're talking about, and a *unit fraction* (new vocabulary) is when we are talking about just one piece. A unit fraction is one piece of the whole that has been partitioned into equal-sized pieces.

Wrap Up

1. **Check for Understanding:** Use manipulatives or sketches to show students a whole partitioned into equal-sized pieces. Ask students to write the unit fraction that describes each of those pieces. Repeat three times.

2. **Connect to Grade-Level Content:** Explicitly connect equivalent fractions to your current grade-level content, during both small group and whole-class time.

Comparing Fractions With Mental Strategies

Focus on Math: In this activity, students connect comparing fractions to your current grade-level content.

Identify Student Strengths: Prior to this activity, identify students' strengths and growth points by using the "Comparing Fractions" prompt (p. 190) or something similar. Use student strengths to connect to new learning.

Materials:

- *Comparing Fractions With Mental Strategies* (Activity Sheet 10.2). Available on the companion website at resources.corwin.com/mathsmallgroups.
- Three note cards with the following fractions written on them: card 1, $\frac{1}{1}$ and $\frac{3}{1}$; card 2, $\frac{2}{5}$ and $\frac{2}{3}$; and card 3, $\frac{5}{8}$ and $\frac{2}{5}$.
- Fraction piece manipulatives with no fractions written on them (circles, squares, bars, pattern blocks, etc.)
- Dry-erase boards and markers or paper and pencils

Create Pathways:

Launch

1. Distribute copies of *Comparing Fractions With Mental Strategies*.
2. Discuss the "Three Ways to Compare Fractions" portion of the activity sheet. (*Note*: This lesson should follow lessons in which students explore each of these methods separately.) Prompts include the following:
   - More of the same-sized pieces
   - Same number of different-sized pieces
   - More than $\frac{1}{2}$ or less than $\frac{1}{2}$
3. Use the three prepared notecards to decide which of the ways to compare fractions fits each example. Use fraction piece manipulatives or sketches to compare.
4. Remind students that when comparing two fractions, they must both be referring to the same-sized whole.

Explore

1. Have students work with a partner to cut out the cards on *Comparing Fractions With Mental Strategies.*

2. Instruct students to sort the fraction pair cards into the three groups using the provided labels (more of the same-sized pieces, same number of different-sized pieces, and more than $\frac{1}{2}$ or less than $\frac{1}{2}$).

3. Use prompting and probing questions to support the students, such as the following:

   - How do you know which group to put this fraction pair card in?

   - Do they have the same number of pieces? (If they are not sure, ask students to build or sketch the two fractions.)

   - Do they have the same number of pieces, but the pieces are different sizes? (If they are not sure, ask students to build or sketch the two fractions.)

   - Is one of the fractions greater than a benchmark and the other less than a benchmark? (If they are not sure, ask students to build or sketch the two fractions.)

Discuss

1. Use the same prompting and probing questions to facilitate a conversation about comparing fraction pairs.

2. Elicit student explanations for each of the prompts. Remind them that they should ask themselves these questions when comparing fractions, in this order, before trying to use more complex methods.

Wrap Up

1. **Check for Understanding:** Use the same three cards prepared for the Launch. Ask students to pick one card at a time and tell which prompt that card matches.

2. **Connect to Grade-Level Content:** Explicitly connect comparing fractions to your current grade-level content, during both small group and whole-class time.

ACTIVITY 10.3

Equivalent Fractions

Focus on Math: In this activity, students connect equivalent fractions to your current grade-level content.

Identify Student Strengths: Prior to this activity, identify students' strengths and growth points by using the "Equivalent Fractions" prompt (p. 190) or something similar. Use student strengths to connect to new learning.

Materials:

- Fraction piece manipulatives with no fractions written on them (circles, squares, bars, pattern blocks, etc.)
- Dry-erase boards and markers or paper and pencils

Create Pathways:

Launch

1. Pose this scenario to students: Kris and Carlos had same-sized pizzas for lunch. Kris said she has $\frac{2}{8}$ of her pizza left, and Carlos said he has $\frac{1}{4}$ of his pizza left. Kris said, "Hey! I have more than you!" Is she correct? How do you know?

2. Discuss the scenario by having students share what they know and what they need to find out.

Explore

1. Have students use fraction pieces to build and then sketch to show how much pizza each person has left.

2. Use prompting and probing questions to help students recognize that Kris is wrong since both of them have the same amount of pizza.
   - Did Kris and Carlos have same-sized pizzas to begin with?
   - Did Kris and Carlos cut their pizzas into same-sized pieces?
   - What do you know about the size of Kris's pieces and the size of Carlos's pieces?
   - How many pieces from Kris's pizza will fit on top of one of Carlos's pieces?

Discuss

1. Use the following questions to discuss the scenario:
   - What was Kris noticing?
   - What was Carlos noticing?
   - What feedback might you give to Kris?
   - What feedback might you give to Carlos?

Wrap Up

1. **Check for Understanding:** Show the fractions $\frac{2}{3}$ and $\frac{1}{6}$. Ask students to illustrate these two fractions using same-sized wholes. Are these equivalent?

2. **Connect to Grade-Level Content:** Explicitly connect unit fractions to your current grade-level content, during both small group and whole-class time.

YOUR TURN

Throughout this chapter, you had the chance to view math small groups through the lens of the Math Small Groups Framework. You focused on the math in the Fraction Foundations standards, looking at ways to identify strengths and planning for learning pathways. Now it's your turn. Take a moment to reflect on the following questions, focusing on how math small groups will benefit the teaching and learning in your classroom.

Learning Intention

After reading this chapter, you will understand how to target the math, identify strengths, and plan pathways for content related to Fraction Foundations.

Success Criteria

You will be able to use the math content trajectory for Fraction Foundations, in addition to your State Standards Framework or the *Math Small Group* Standards Trajectory Document, to help you identify the just-right starting place for your students.

The *Math Small Group* Standards Trajectory Document offers a map that shows how all the standards for each domain interrelate. To download this tool, visit resources. corwin.com/mathsmallgroups.

- What ideas did you glean from this chapter that will help you engage in the three steps of the Math Small Group Framework?
- What did you learn about the pathway of Fraction Foundations across grade levels? How will this help you as you work with your students in the math small group setting?

CHAPTER 11

FRACTION OPERATIONS

> ### Learning Intention
>
> After reading this chapter, you will understand how to target the math, identify strengths, and plan pathways for content related to Fraction Operations.
>
> ### Success Criteria
>
> You will be able to use the math content trajectory for Fraction Operations, in addition to your State Standards Framework or the *Math Small Group* Standards Trajectory Document, to help you identify the just-right starting place for your students.

CHAPTER INTRODUCTION

Although typically addressed in Grades 4–5, Fraction Operations are informally introduced in earlier grades as students approach their major grade-level work of partitioning shapes, combining unit fractions, and skip counting by fractions. These processes are formalized in later grades as students put together ideas such as equivalence and behaviors of the operations to formalize their work with Fraction Operations.

In this chapter, we will take a glimpse at what it means to work on Fraction Operations in your teacher-facilitated math small groups. This chapter covers a lot of content, simply providing a few examples for how you might approach this work at different points in time. Quite often, show-and-tell teaching emerges when we teach Fraction Operations. This can occur for a variety of reasons, including the need for us to further develop our understanding of the specific content knowledge related to teaching Fraction Operations conceptually.

As you read this chapter, take some time to reflect on your own understandings and the ways in which you explain Fraction Operations. If needed, practice your representations and explanations ahead of time to ensure that you are able to explain these ideas simply and clearly. And, as always, take care to continue encouraging student voice in your math small groups rather than resorting to show-and-tell teaching.

FRACTION OPERATIONS: AN OVERVIEW

For the purposes of this book, the trajectories for fraction addition and subtraction and fraction multiplication and division have been separated so you can clearly see how each progresses on its own. Please keep in mind that when you are working on these math concepts with your small groups, they are very much interconnected, especially in the ways in which they use foundational ideas such as unit fractions and equivalent fractions. Also note that fractions are typically inclusive of improper fractions and mixed numbers across the grades.

Taking a look at the addition and subtraction trajectory first, you'll notice that the big foundational piece right at the beginning is fraction foundations as sums of unit fractions. This relates closely to, and should be tightly aligned with, the first standard in the multiplication and division trajectory: understand a fraction as a multiple of the unit fraction. This connection is similar to the connection of whole-number repeated addition and beginning equal groups multiplication.

It's important to note that in most State Standards Frameworks, the addition/subtraction trajectory spans three grade levels. After working with unit fractions in third grade, fourth graders use decomposing strategies to add and subtract. Then, finally, in fifth grade, they use equivalent fraction strategies to add and subtract.

Similarly, the multiplication and division trajectory spans multiple years, typically fourth and fifth grades. As with addition and subtraction, students begin by using unit fractions as part of their multiplication work. They use this understanding to multiply fractions and whole numbers, and then to understand that multiplication can also be interpreted as scaling, giving students the challenge of redefining multiplication. Up until this point, multiplication always made quantities bigger, but with this new lens, students see that multiplying by a fraction makes quantities smaller. They can then use this new understanding to multiply whole numbers by fractions; fractions by whole numbers; and, eventually, fractions by fractions.

As students near the end of the K–5 Fraction Operations trajectory, they use what they've learned to divide whole numbers by fractions and fractions by whole numbers, and the rest of fraction division is typically left until Grade 6.

In Chapter 4, we discussed the Math Small Group Framework. The content in the rest of this chapter will follow the structure of the framework, pictured again in Figure 11.1.

Figure 11.1 • *Teacher-Facilitated Math Small Group Framework*

STEP 1 Focus on Math	• Deconstruct grade-level standard(s) of focus • Study the corresponding K-6 standards trajectory • Identify pathway concepts/skills that connect to grade-level standards • Collect formative data based on the learning pathway

STEP 2 Identify Strengths	• Identify teacher strengths
	• Identify learner strengths
	   ○ What's the last thing students understand along the learning pathway?
	   ○ How do they engage with, represent, and express their learning?

STEP 3 Create Pathways	• Use the Explore Before Explain (Eb4E) approach • Ascertain what students *do* know • Connect small group work and whole-class learning in both settings

FOCUS ON MATH: MATH CONTENT TRAJECTORIES FOR FRACTION OPERATIONS

For this first step, Focus on Math, you will want to go through four processes to ensure you identify the necessary content for your students. Fraction Operations spans Grades 4–5 and includes foundational ideas from Grades K–3.

The four processes to engage in as you Focus on Math are as follows:

1. Identify and deconstruct the grade-level standard(s) relevant to Fraction Operations.

2. Study the Fraction Operations standards trajectory in this chapter (see Figure 11.2) as well as in the *Math Small Group* Standards Trajectory Document.

3. Identify the multigrade-level pathway concepts and skills that connect to on-grade-level standards for Fraction Operations. This may include standards from previous grade levels as well as standards for future grade levels. Use whichever standards you need based on the structure (heterogeneous, Guided Math, etc.) and goals for your math small groups.

4. Collect formative data based on the Fraction Operations standards. Your formative data may include daily entrance or exit tickets, weekly common formative assessments, classroom observational data, or any other data you collect on a regular basis.

Figure 11.2 • *Trajectories for Fraction Operations*

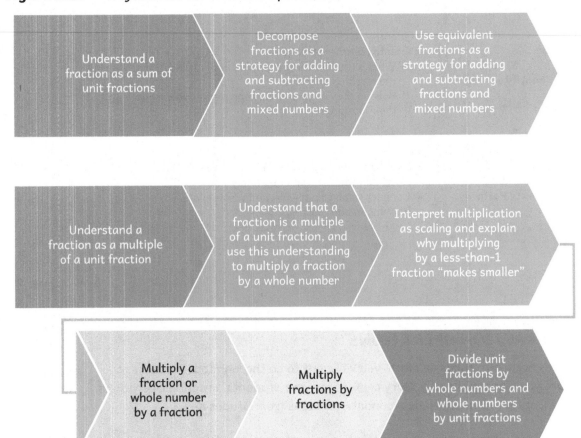

Algebraic Thinking and Overarching Structures

These standards trajectories include several overarching mathematical themes as well. They don't generally fall in a specific place along the trajectories; rather, they appear in several places along the learning continuum, both within and across grade levels. Often, these standards can be used to connect big ideas across domains and grades because they appear so frequently.

Patterns and Generalizations

As you can see in these trajectories, unit fractions play a powerful role in both fraction sense and all four operations. This is definitely a big idea to embed into your Math Small Group Framework. In addition, interpreting multiplication as scaling is yet another big idea that plays a huge role in middle school and high school mathematics. Developing this notion at the conceptual level is critical for students' future success, so it is important to target it as well.

Properties

Again, even though the properties of operations are not mentioned in the fraction domains for most State Standards Frameworks, it is important to connect all of the properties for both addition and multiplication into your math small groups as well as make explicit connections back to your whole group instruction.

Strategies and Representations

Be sure to continue the word problem situation types used with whole-number operations. Students should still be engaging with different word problem situation types. See the tables in Chapters 8 and 9 for more guidance on the word problem situations. Continue to use letters as symbols for the unknown numbers and reinforce the meaning of the = sign as a relationship symbol rather than an action symbol. Also continue to reinforce the use of mental computation and estimation strategies, including benchmark fractions and fraction sense. Students will benefit greatly if you attend to these broader ideas when creating the learning pathways for your math small groups.

MATH TOOLS TO SUPPORT THESE TRAJECTORIES

When preparing for your math small groups, you may be planning for math concepts and skills that are not necessarily at your grade level. The suggestions in this section are intended to help you think through the materials you may need, especially for facilitating conceptual development.

As you gather materials, be mindful that you include a wide variety to encourage students to translate within and across the different categories of representations: concrete (manipulatives and objects), visual, symbolic, verbal, and contextual (Lesh et al., 1987). You should encourage students to represent their thinking in ways that make sense to them, giving them choice as much as possible. In addition, ask students to work side by side with different representations and then compare and contrast what they see. This will help students make sense of their thinking as well as develop new ways of thinking about the concepts and skills at hand.

See Chapter 2 for more information about the Lesh Translation Model of Representations.

Concrete Representations

Providing students with a variety of fraction models helps them generate flexibility with defining the unit, or "whole," in a variety of ways. You can use commercial, virtual, or homemade fraction manipulatives, including fraction circles, squares, tiles/bars, and towers. You can also use Cuisenaire® rods or pattern blocks to explore fractional relationships (see Object 11.1). Or, you may simply want to use paper shapes, asking your students to cut or fold paper shapes into same-sized fraction pieces (Moore & Rimbey, 2021).

> Note that when working with commercial fraction pieces, students will be better off with fraction pieces that have no markings on them. That way, the "whole" can be redefined depending on the operations and number sets.

Object 11.1 · *Common Fraction Piece Manipulatives (fraction bars, Cuisenaire® rods, pattern blocks)*

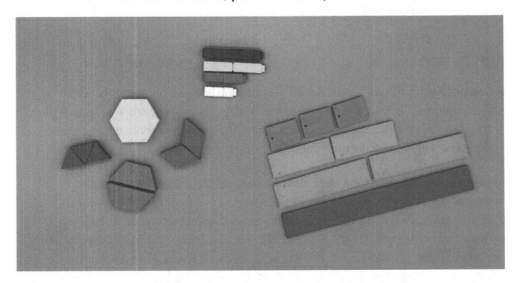

Visual Representations

Having students sketch their fraction work will increase the likelihood that it will transfer to long-term memory. Students typically sketch objects similar to the fraction pieces illustrated in Object 11.1. Provide them with plenty of writing materials so they can use color to support their thinking about fractions. Color makes a big difference when your students are trying to represent ideas such as fractional parts of fractional parts.

Symbolic Representations

Far too frequently, students learn Fraction Operations procedurally first, and then we try to backtrack to the conceptual ideas. That is the opposite of what students need to become fluid with fraction ideas. Invite students to use fraction notation to clarify their sketches, but in the stages where you are developing conceptual understanding, avoid having them notate Fraction Operations in a procedural fashion.

Verbal Representations

Sentence Starters: Think ahead about what kinds of prompts you might provide to students to get them talking about Fraction Operations. Create an anchor chart or a set of cards on a binder ring that provide sentence starters for students, such as the following:

- I need same-sized wholes to add fractions because . . .
- I need same-sized pieces to add fractions because . . .
- I need same-sized pieces to subtract fractions because . . .
- Equivalent fractions help me when . . .
- I can use the word "of" for multiplication because . . .
- Fraction division behaves like whole-number multiplication because . . .

Verbal Explanations: When students are working with Fraction Operations, ask them to explain and describe their thinking. This might include asking them to whisper-talk to themselves as they describe the steps they're using to multiply and divide. Sometimes, saying things out loud helps us make sense of our own work or realize where we've made an error in our thinking or calculations.

Written Explanations: You may also want to ask students to write about their thinking at different times. Here are two prompts you might want to consider: "What are the steps you used to find your solution?" and "How do you know your solution is correct? Prove it."

Contextual Representations

Teacher-Created Context Problems: Whenever possible, provide context to help students engage with Fraction Operations. Use people, places, and situations that are of high interest to your students, specifically, or to their age group, generally.

Student-Created Context Problems: Ask students to create their own contexts to demonstrate fraction understanding. You provide the symbolic representations, and students compose the word problem. This can bring a bit of playfulness into your small groups, allowing students to make their own connections between math and the real world. It also provides you with insights into their understanding of the behaviors of fractions.

Recording Materials

Provide a variety of recording materials for students to use, including blank paper, dry-erase boards, markers, colored pencils, pencils, and erasers.

IDENTIFY STRENGTHS: SAMPLE PROMPTS FOR DETECTING LEARNERS' CONTENT STRENGTHS

Identifying strengths regarding Fraction Operations includes finding out what students already know about multiplicative thinking.

Keep in mind that identifying strengths includes a focus on both you and your students.

1. **Identify teacher strengths:** How do you talk about Fraction Operations conceptually? What fraction-specific representations do you use to demonstrate each of the operations? Can you explain the operations simply and in a way that makes sense without using formal algorithms? How do you include the use of equivalent fractions without a formal algorithm for finding equivalent fractions?

2. **Identify learner strengths:** Use the formative data you've collected as well as the sample prompts that follow to determine learner strengths. What's the last thing students *do* understand along the learning pathway? How do they engage with, represent, and express their learning?

The goal of using these prompts is to identify the last thing the student knows about this particular concept or skill. This will be the starting place for your math small group work, building on successes and connecting to new learning. This provides valuable information as you plan for your teacher-facilitated math small groups.

Decomposing Fractions as an Addition Strategy

Ask students to decompose the fraction $\frac{5}{4}$ into wholes and fractions (e.g., you're looking for $\frac{4}{4}$ and $\frac{1}{4}$). If successful, ask students to add $3\frac{1}{4}$ and $4\frac{1}{4}$. If successful again, ask students to use what they know about decomposing a fraction to find the sum of $2\frac{3}{4}$ and $1\frac{2}{4}$. Record your students' successes and growth points. You can repeat using other fractions.

Using Unit Fractions as a Multiplication Strategy

Ask students to sketch 3 × 4. Next, ask students to sketch $3 \times \frac{1}{4}$. Finally ask students whether $3 \times \frac{1}{4}$ is the same amount as $\frac{3}{4}$. Why or why not? Record your students' successes and growth points. You can repeat using other numbers.

Interpreting Multiplication as Scaling

Ask students to sketch 3 × 4 = 12 using an equal groups model. Next, ask students to sketch 3 × 4 = 12 using lines or bar models to show that 12 is 3 times longer than 4. Finally, ask them what is similar and what is different between those two models. Record your students' successes and growth points. (*Note:* This is a prerequisite for multiplying with fractions, leading to understanding that when you multiply by a fraction, the total scale is smaller than the amount you begin with.) You can repeat using other numbers.

CREATE PATHWAYS: SAMPLE TEACHER-FACILITATED SMALL GROUP LESSONS

When creating learning pathways, consider what you've learned about student strengths as starting points to build upon.

The three components for Creating Pathways are as follows:

▶ Use the Explore Before Explain (Eb4E) Lesson Planning Template to plan your lesson.

▶ Consider what you learned about your students' strengths—what do they already know about Fraction Operations?

▶ Connect Fraction Operations concepts between your math small group work and whole-class learning. Use Fraction Operations routines in both settings to help students make connections.

> To download the Eb4E Lesson Planning Template, visit resources.corwin.com/mathsmallgroups.

The following selected sample lessons provide examples for how you might design a math small group lesson, attending to each area of the framework. Note that these examples can be easily adapted for students working with all number sets.

Adding Parts to Parts— It's Part-y Time!

Focus on Math: In this activity, students connect decomposing fractions as an addition strategy to your current grade-level content.

Identify Student Strengths: Prior to this activity, identify students' strengths and growth points by using the "Decomposing Fractions as an Addition Strategy" prompt (p. 206) or something similar. Use student strengths to connect to new learning.

Materials:

- Fraction piece manipulatives with no fractions written on them (circles, squares, bars, pattern blocks, etc.)
- Dry-erase boards and markers or paper and pencils

Create Pathways:

Launch

1. Pose the following scenario: Maria's mom made mini-cakes for her birthday. They cut each cake into four slices. When the party was over, there was $\frac{5}{4}$ of a cake left. What did this look like?
2. Have students show the scenario with fraction pieces or sketches.
3. Use prompting and probing questions to help the students see that $\frac{5}{4}$ can be represented by decomposing it into $\frac{4}{4}$ and $\frac{1}{4}$, which is the same as $1\frac{1}{4}$.

Explore

1. Divide students into pairs.
2. Pose the following scenario: The next day, Maria's mom made mini-cakes for her brother's party. After his party, there were $2\frac{3}{4}$ cakes in the kitchen and $1\frac{3}{4}$ cakes on the table outside. How many cakes were left over altogether?
3. Instruct students to use fraction pieces, sketches, and symbols to solve.
4. Use prompting and probing questions such as the following to help the students find the sum using decomposing fractions as a strategy:
   - How might you combine like terms to add these two numbers (e.g., whole numbers and fractions)?

- How many whole cakes were left?
- How much cake was there when you combine the cut-up cakes?
- How might you use what you know about decomposing fractions to find the total?

Discuss

1. Have students share their work.

2. Ask prompting and probing questions to support students in making connections between the different representations:

   - How did you know which numbers to put together to get started?
   - What did you do when you encountered an improper fraction?

Wrap Up

1. **Check for Understanding:** Have students use sketches or numbers to add $2\frac{3}{5} + 3\frac{1}{5}$. Ask them to use what they know about decomposing fractions to find the total. You may continue with the cake context if that is helpful.

2. **Connect to Grade-Level Content:** Explicitly connect decomposing fractions as an addition strategy to your current grade-level content, during both small group and whole-class time.

ACTIVITY 11.2

Multiplying Pieces

Focus on Math: In this activity, students connect using unit fractions as a multiplication strategy to your current grade-level content.

Identify Student Strengths: Prior to this activity, identify students' strengths and growth points by using the "Using Unit Fractions as a Multiplication Strategy" prompt (p. 206) or something similar. Use student strengths to connect to new learning.

Materials:

- Counters
- Fraction piece manipulatives with no fractions written on them (circles, squares, bars, pattern blocks, etc.)
- Dry-erase boards and markers or paper and pencils

Create Pathways:

Launch

1. Have students use sketches or counters to model 3 × 4 and explain what this means (e.g., 3 groups with 4 in each group).
2. Have students use sketches or fraction pieces to show $3 \times \frac{1}{4}$.
3. Ask students to explain how their model of 3 × 4 is similar to and different from their model of $3 \times \frac{1}{4}$.
4. Ask students whether $3 \times \frac{1}{4}$ is the same amount as $\frac{3}{4}$. Why or why not?
5. Use prompting and probing questions to help them see that this is, indeed, the same amount.
6. Have students create a context that helps them remember this idea. For example, they may say that if they have 3 one-fourth-sized apple pieces left from a bag and they put them all together, they would have $\frac{3}{4}$ of an apple. If helpful, have students create two or three additional contexts.

Explore

1. Divide students into pairs.
2. Have students work together to use a context to help them show that one can use multiplication of unit fractions to show how a fraction is composed.

3. Pose fractions for them to work with, such as $\frac{2}{3}$, $\frac{3}{5}$, $\frac{5}{6}$, and $\frac{5}{8}$. Have students use fraction pieces, sketches, and numbers to show their work.

4. Remind students that they must always define the whole when working with fractions.

Discuss

1. Select one fraction that all pairs complete.

2. Have pairs share their work with the others in the math small group.

3. Use prompting and probing questions to help them use correct vocabulary and to correctly use their selected contexts:

   - Listen to how I say this: "The fraction $\frac{5}{8}$ has 5 one-eighth-sized pieces." What does that mean? How might you write that as a multiplication expression?

   - Can you describe another fraction by naming the number of same-sized pieces? How do you write that as a multiplication expression?

Wrap Up

1. **Check for Understanding:** Ask students to rewrite $\frac{1}{5}$ as a multiplication of unit fractions and to use a context to explain, in writing, why these are different ways to show the same amount.

2. **Connect to Grade-Level Content:** Explicitly connect using unit fractions as a multiplication strategy to your current grade-level content, during both small group and whole-class time.

ACTIVITY 11.3

Multiplying Your Efforts

Focus on Math: In this activity, students connect interpreting multiplication as scaling to your current grade-level content.

Identify Student Strengths: Prior to this activity, identify students' strengths and growth points by using the "Interpreting Multiplication as Scaling" prompt (p. 207) or something similar. Use student strengths to connect to new learning.

Materials:

- Cuisenaire® rods
- Dry-erase boards and markers or paper and pencils

Create Pathways:

Launch

1. Have students sketch 3 × 4 = 12 using an equal groups model.
2. Have students sketch 3 × 4 = 12 using lines or bar models to show that 12 is 3 times longer than 4.
3. Use prompting and probing questions to help students communicate that when they use lines or bar models to show that 12 is 3 times longer than 4, they are comparing 4 and 12 using multiplication:
   - What is the total length of the long piece?
   - What is the size of the short piece you're comparing?
   - How many of the same-sized short pieces do you need to make the same length as the long piece?
   - How might you describe that relationship using a multiplication expression?

Explore

1. Divide students into pairs.
2. Pose the following scenario: Ana and Jamal are making gift bows in their art class. Ana has 3 times more ribbon than Jamal. If Jamal has 5 feet of ribbon, how much does Ana have?
3. Have students work in pairs to show this comparison. They should use Cuisenaire® rods, sketches, and/or numbers to show their thinking.

Discuss

1. Ask students to show and explain their thinking to the group.

2. Use prompting and probing questions to help students realize that thinking about multiplication as comparison is important as they get ready to multiply fractions:

   - What did you notice about how we used multiplication to compare?

   - How do the two factors work together to describe the comparison?

   - Can you explain the comparison without using multiplication language (times, multiple, factor, multiplication, etc.)?

Wrap Up

1. **Check for Understanding:** Have students sketch a number line or bar model to show $4 \times 2 = 8$ (8 is 4 times longer than 2).

2. **Connect to Grade-Level Content:** Explicitly connect interpreting multiplication as scaling to your current grade-level content, during both small group and whole-class time.

YOUR TURN

Throughout this chapter, you had the chance to view math small groups through the lens of the Math Small Group Framework. You focused on the math in the Fraction Operations standards, looking at ways to identify strengths and planning for learning pathways. Now it's your turn. Take a moment to reflect on the questions that follow, focusing on how math small groups will benefit the teaching and learning in your classroom.

Learning Intention

After reading this chapter, you will understand how to target the math, identify strengths, and plan pathways for content related to Fraction Operations.

Success Criteria

You will be able to use the math content trajectory for Fraction Operations, in addition to your State Standards Framework or the *Math Small Group* Standards Trajectory Document, to help you identify the just-right starting place for your students.

The *Math Small Group* Standards Trajectory Document offers a map that shows how all the standards for each domain interrelate. To download this tool, visit resources. corwin.com/mathsmallgroups.

- What ideas did you glean from this chapter that will help you engage in the three steps of the Math Small Group Framework?
- What did you learn about the pathway of Fraction Operations across grade levels? How will this help you as you work with your students in the math small group setting?

CHAPTER 12

FRACTION AND DECIMAL CONNECTIONS

Learning Intention

After reading this chapter, you will understand how to target the math, identify strengths, and plan pathways for content related to Fraction and Decimal Connections.

Success Criteria

You will be able to use the math content trajectory for Fraction and Decimal Connections, in addition to your State Standards Framework or the *Math Small Group* Standards Trajectory Document, to help you identify the just-right starting place for your students.

CHAPTER INTRODUCTION

Far too often, decimal foundations and operations are taught exclusively as part of the base-ten trajectory, neglecting the notion that decimal fractions are fractions, too. However, it's important that decimal fractions be taught as the base-ten notation of fractions. For example, 0.7 and $\frac{7}{10}$ represent the same amount, but many students remain unaware of this simple truth.

Furthermore, you will want to be sure your students have a full understanding of the basic concepts of working with decimal numbers. As pictured in Object 12.1, even the "anatomy" of a decimal number often remains elusive for your students. Your students need to know that

▶ a "decimal" is any base-ten number.

▶ the "dot" that appears between the whole number and the decimal fraction is called a "decimal point," not simply a decimal.

▶ the decimal point simply separates the whole number from the decimal fraction.

▶ a decimal number with digits on both sides of the decimal point is a mixed number, just like a mixed number written in fraction form.

▶ the "point of symmetry" for a decimal number is not the decimal point—it is the digit in the ones place.

Object 12.1 · *The Anatomy of a Decimal*

Taking time to introduce and reinforce these ideas with your students will help them internalize the connections between fraction and decimal notation, and it will promote the idea that mathematics is connected and coherent.

FRACTION AND DECIMAL CONNECTIONS: AN OVERVIEW

This work with decimal fractions typically appears near the end of our K–5 trajectory. In most State Standards Frameworks, the work culminates in sixth grade, leaving it incomplete at the end of the K–5 continuum. In fact, in most states, decimal fraction work does not begin until fourth grade. This may be problematic for some, since the decimal point is often introduced earlier in money units. Talking about the decimal point as the separation between the whole number and the fraction would be useful in these early grades as well.

When targeting the math in this trajectory, consider making a strong connection between fraction and decimal representations. That is a big idea in most states' fourth-grade standards frameworks, so be sure to continue making that connection. One important idea, hinted at earlier, is that the decimal point is simply the mark that divides the whole number from the fraction.

As shown in Object 12.2, a decimal can be composed of three parts: the whole number, the decimal point, and the decimal fraction. Note that the word "decimal" simply refers to any base-ten number, even if it is just a whole number. When all three parts of the decimal appear, you are looking at what is, in essence, a mixed number. When the mixed number is written in fraction form, as you see on the right, the decimal point is unnecessary because the eye can easily distinguish between the whole number and the fraction. However, when a number is written in decimal form, the decimal point is necessary to make the distinction between the whole number and the decimal fraction. Ensuring students understand the connection between decimal notation and fraction notation gives them a stronger sense of the cohesion in our number system.

Object 12.2 · *Comparison Between a Decimal and a Mixed Number*

$$3.45 = 3\frac{45}{100}$$

We typically teach decimal operations conceptually in Grades 4–5, leaving formal algorithm work to be completed in middle school. As you work with decimal operations conceptually, it is important to consider that decimal fractions behave as both base-ten numbers and fractions. Although most curriculum resources address decimal operations as extensions of base-ten operations, using fraction language during the conceptual stages helps students gain a stronger foundation.

In Chapter 4, we discussed the Math Small Group Framework. The content in the rest of this chapter will follow the structure of the framework, pictured again in Figure 12.1.

Figure 12.1 · *Teacher-Facilitated Math Small Group Framework*

STEP 1 **Focus on Math**	• Deconstruct grade-level standard(s) of focus • Study the corresponding K-6 standards trajectory • Identify pathway concepts/skills that connect to grade-level standards • Collect formative data based on the learning pathway

STEP 2
Identify Strengths
	• Identify teacher strengths
	• Identify learner strengths
	  ○ What's the last thing students understand along the learning pathway?
	  ○ How do they engage with, represent, and express their learning?

STEP 3 **Create Pathways**	• Use the Explore Before Explain (Eb4E) approach • Ascertain what students *do* know • Connect small group work and whole-class learning in both settings

FOCUS ON MATH: MATH CONTENT TRAJECTORY FOR FRACTION AND DECIMAL CONNECTIONS

For this first step, Focus on Math, you will want to go through four processes to ensure you identify the necessary content for your students. Fraction and Decimal Connections spans Grades 4–5 and includes foundational ideas from Grades 1–3.

The four processes to engage in as you Focus on Math are as follows:

1. Identify and deconstruct the grade-level standard(s) relevant to Fraction and Decimal Connections.

2. Study the Fraction and Decimal Connections standards trajectory in this chapter (see Figure 12.2) as well as in the *Math Small Group* Standards Trajectory Document.

3. Identify the multigrade-level pathway concepts and skills that connect to on-grade-level standards for Fraction and Decimal Connections. This may include standards from previous grade levels as well as standards for future grade levels. Use whichever standards you need based on the structure (heterogeneous, Guided Math, etc.) and goals for your math small groups.

4. Collect formative data based on the Fraction and Decimal Connections standards. Your formative data may include daily entrance or exit tickets, weekly common formative assessments, classroom observational data, or any other data you collect on a regular basis.

Figure 12.2 • *Trajectory for Fraction and Decimal Connections*

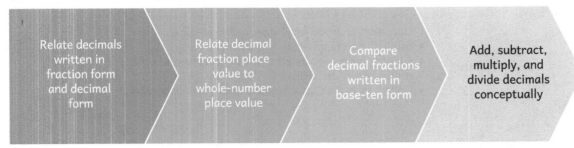

Algebraic Thinking and Overarching Structures

This standards trajectory includes several overarching themes as well. They don't generally fall in a specific place along the trajectory; rather, they appear in several places along the learning continuum, both within and across grade levels. Often, these standards can be used to connect big ideas across domains and grades because they appear so frequently.

Patterns and Generalizations

Frequently, connect fraction notation and base-ten notation for decimal fractions (see Object 12.3). Students need to internalize that decimal fractions are a subset of all fractions and that there are multiple ways of representing them.

Object 12.3 · *Connecting Base-Ten Notation and Fraction Notation*

$$0.05 = \frac{5}{100}$$

$$0.89 = \frac{89}{100}$$

$$3.45 = 3\frac{45}{100}$$

Place Value

Because decimal fractions are written in place value form, help students make connections to whole-number place value. Frequently, students have an underdeveloped sense of place value to the right of the decimal point because they do not spend enough time integrating new understanding to what they already know about place value and fractions. Continue to reinforce the ideas of grouping and ungrouping tens, emphasizing the nesting nature of place value on both sides of the decimal point.

Properties

Continue to connect the commutative, associative, and identity properties for both addition and multiplication as well as the distributive property for multiplication. Students likely need reminders that these properties have a role to play with every number set.

Strategies and Representations

Just as with all other number sets, continue to target the different word problem situation types discussed in Chapters 8 and 9.

MATH TOOLS TO SUPPORT THIS TRAJECTORY

When preparing for your math small groups, you may be planning for math concepts and skills that are not necessarily at your grade level. The suggestions in this section are intended to help you think through the materials you may need, especially for facilitating conceptual development.

As you gather materials, be mindful that you include a wide variety to encourage students to translate within and across the different categories of representations: concrete (manipulatives and objects), visual, symbolic, verbal, and contextual (Lesh et al., 1987). You should encourage students to represent their thinking in ways that make sense to them, giving them choice as much as possible. In addition, ask students to work side by side with different representations and then compare and contrast what they see. This will help students make sense of their thinking as well as develop new ways of thinking about the concepts and skills at hand.

> See Chapter 2 for more information about the Lesh Translation Model of Representations.

Concrete Representations

Base-Ten Manipulatives: As with whole-number operations, groupable manipulatives provide the best option for helping students fully grasp the nesting nature of place value and its impact on operations. If base-ten blocks are your only option, you may choose to either use virtual base-ten blocks or have your students work with preprinted hundreds grids.

When using base-ten manipulatives for decimal concepts, the important idea is to identify the "unit" that can be decomposed into fractional pieces. With base-ten blocks, this often means identifying the flat as one whole, making the rods tenths, and the units hundredths (see Object 12.4).

Object 12.4 · *Using Base-Ten Blocks and KP® Ten-Frame Tiles to Represent Decimal Fractions*

Visual Representations

Sketching: Ask students to sketch their representations as much as possible. When it comes to working on decimal operations, grid paper is the best option so students can quickly sketch hundreds grids to use in showing tenths and hundredths.

Symbolic Representations

Conceptual Decimal Operations: When students record their work, encourage them to use symbols to represent various aspects of their conceptual drawings. For example, students should label sketches with equations as well as record the expressions/equations associated with the partial products in an open array diagram (see Object 12.5). Because the K–5 trajectory ends at conceptual development, there should not be a need for you to work with your small groups on standard algorithms.

Object 12.5 · *Student Sketch for Subtraction 3.45 – 2.36*

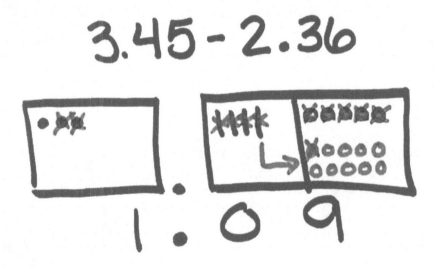

Verbal Representations

Sentence Starters: Think ahead about what kinds of prompts you might provide to students to get them talking about decimal operations. Create an anchor chart or a set of cards on a binder ring that provides sentence starters for your students.

- A decimal is . . .
- A decimal point is . . . And its job is to . . .
- When a number has digits on both sides of the decimal point, that means . . .
- I can call the digits to the right of the decimal point a "decimal fraction" because . . .
- Fractions and decimal fractions are similar because . . .

Verbal Explanations: When small groups are working with whole-number multiplication and division, ask students to explain and describe their thinking. This might include asking them to whisper-talk to themselves as they describe the steps they're using to multiply and divide. Sometimes, saying things out loud helps us make sense of our own work or realize where we've made an error in our thinking or calculations.

Written Explanations: You may also want to ask students to write about their thinking at different times. Here are two prompts you might want to consider: "What are the steps you used to find your solution?" and "How do you know your solution is correct? Prove it."

Contextual Representations

Teacher-Created Context Problems: Whenever possible, provide context to help students engage with the decimal operations. Use people, places, and situations that are of high interest to your students, specifically, or to their age group, generally.

Student-Created Context Problems: Ask students to create their own contexts for the multiplication and division problems. You provide the expression or equation, and students compose the word problem. This can bring a bit of playfulness into your small groups, allowing students to make their own connections between math and the real world. It also provides you with insights into their understanding of the behaviors of multiplication and division.

Recording Materials

Provide a variety of recording materials for students to use, including blank paper, dry-erase boards, markers, colored pencils, pencils, and erasers.

IDENTIFY STRENGTHS: SAMPLE PROMPTS FOR DETECTING LEARNERS' CONTENT STRENGTHS

Identifying strengths regarding Fraction and Decimal Connections includes finding out what students already know about multiplicative thinking.

Keep in mind that identifying strengths includes focusing on both you and your students.

1. **Identify teacher strengths:** Can you meaningfully talk about the connection between decimal notation and fraction notation? How do you represent decimal fractions conceptually? How do you explain the process of "ungrouping" one whole into tenths and tenths into hundredths?

2. **Identify learner strengths:** Use the formative data you've collected as well as the sample prompts that follow to determine learner

strengths. What's the last thing students *do* understand along the learning pathway? How do they engage with, represent, and express their learning?

The goal of using these prompts is to identify the last thing the students know about this particular concept or skill. This will be the starting place for your math small group work, building on successes and connecting to new learning. This provides valuable information as you plan for your teacher-facilitated math small groups.

Relating Decimal and Fraction Notations

Ask students to write the following numbers in fraction form: $\frac{3}{100}, \frac{67}{100}, \frac{30}{100}$. Next, ask students to write those same numbers in decimal form. Finally, ask students to use base-ten manipulatives to represent each of those fractions. Record students' successes and growth points.

Comparing Decimal Fractions

Ask students to write 0.3 and 0.4 and circle the one that is greater. Ask students to write 0.67 and 0.76 and circle the one that is greater. Ask students to write 0.03 and 0.3 and circle the one that is greater. Record students' successes and growth points.

Multiplying Decimal Fractions

Ask students to sketch 3×4. Next, ask students to sketch 3×0.4. Finally, ask students to sketch 3×0.04. Ask students to explain what is similar and what is different about each of these situations. Record students' successes and growth points.

CREATE PATHWAYS: SAMPLE TEACHER-FACILITATED SMALL GROUP LESSONS

When creating learning pathways, consider what you've learned about student strengths as starting points to build upon.

The three components for Creating Pathways are as follows:

► Use the Explore Before Explain (Eb4E) Lesson Planning Template to plan your lesson.

► Consider what you learned about your students' strengths—what do they already know about Fraction and Decimal Connections?

► Connect Fraction and Decimal Connections concepts between your math small group work and whole-class learning. Use Base-Ten Place Value routines in both settings to help students make connections.

To download the Eb4E Lesson Planning Template, visit resources.corwin.com/mathsmallgroups.

The following selected sample lessons provide examples for how you might design a math small group lesson, attending to each area of the framework. Note that these examples can be easily adapted for students working with all number sets.

Decimals Are Fractions, Too!

Focus on Math: In this activity, students connect the relationships between decimal and fraction notations to your current grade-level content.

Identify Student Strengths: Prior to this activity, identify students' strengths and growth points by using the "Relating Decimal and Fraction Notations" prompt (p. 224) or something similar. Use student strengths to connect to new learning.

Materials:

- Base-ten blocks, KP® Ten-Frame Tiles, or other base-ten manipulatives
- Dry-erase boards and markers or paper and pencils
- Laminated sheets of graph paper for sketching (*optional*)

Create Pathways:

Launch

1. Have students write $\frac{3}{10}$ in both fraction and decimal form. Support their recordings if they are unsure.
2. Have students make a sketch that shows $\frac{3}{10}$.
3. Discuss that whether they write three-tenths in fraction or decimal form, they both represent the exact same amount. They are simply two ways to write the same amount.

Explore

1. Divide students into pairs.
2. Display the fractions $\frac{7}{10}$, $\frac{67}{100}$, and $\frac{3}{100}$.
3. Have pairs work together to represent each of the numbers in both fraction and decimal notation.
4. Instruct students to also choose a context to illustrate each pair, noting that both notations describe the same amount. They should represent each of the numbers in a different way (manipulatives, sketches, numbers).

Discuss

1. Have pairs share their work with the rest of the group.

2. Ask prompting and probing questions to ensure that each student understands that the fraction and decimal notations describe the same amount:

   - How are fractions and decimal fractions similar?
   - Why is it necessary to include a decimal point with decimal fractions but not with regular fractions?
   - How are 0.3 and 0.03 similar? How are they different? (repeat with any two fractions)

Wrap Up

1. **Check for Understanding:** Ask students to record each of the following in both fraction and decimal notation: nine hundredths, nine tenths, 99 hundredths.

2. **Connect to Grade-Level Content:** Explicitly connect the relationships between decimal and fraction notations to your current grade-level content, during both small group and whole-class time.

Comparing Decimal Fractions

Focus on Math: In this activity, students connect comparing decimal fractions to your current grade-level content.

Identify Student Strengths: Prior to this activity, identify students' strengths and growth points by using the "Comparing Decimal Fractions" prompt (p. 224) or something similar. Use student strengths to connect to new learning.

Materials:

- Base-ten blocks, KP® Ten-Frame Tiles, or other base-ten manipulatives
- Dry-erase boards and markers or paper and pencils
- Laminated sheets of graph paper for sketching (*optional*)
- *Comparing Decimal Fractions* (Activity Sheet 12.2), cut cards apart and place them in a bowl or paper bag ahead of time. Available on the companion website at resources.corwin.com/mathsmallgroups.

Create Pathways:

Launch

1. Have students write 0.5 and 0.6 and sketch or use manipulatives to represent each.
2. Discuss which is lesser and which is greater.
3. Repeat with 0.32 and 0.23.
4. Repeat with 0.1 and 0.01.
5. Each time, ask students to describe which is lesser, which is greater, and why. If needed, review the words *lesser* and *greater*—some students think of *greater* as "better" rather than "more than." Also, remind students that decimal notations such as these are fractions, and we can call these decimal fractions.

Explore

1. Divide students into pairs.
2. Have one student from each pair select a *Comparing Decimal Fractions* card from the bowl or bag.
3. Instruct pairs to each use a different representation (manipulatives, sketches, numbers) to build, sketch, or write the two decimal fractions.

4. Within their pairs, have students discuss how their representations are similar and different and then decide which decimal fraction is greater and which is lesser.

5. Repeat this process until time is up.

Discuss

1. Have students share their work with the group.

2. Use prompting and probing questions as needed to assist students in explaining how they modeled each fraction and how they decided which is greater and which is lesser.

Wrap Up

1. **Check for Understanding:** Ask students to write 0.3 and 0.4 and circle the one that is greater. Ask students to write 0.67 and 0.76 and circle the one that is greater. Ask students to write 0.03 and 0.3 and circle the one that is greater.

2. **Connect to Grade-Level Content:** Explicitly connect comparing decimal fractions to your current grade-level content, during both small group and whole-class time.

ACTIVITY 12.3

Looking for Decimal Patterns

Focus on Math: In this activity, students connect multiplying decimal fractions to your current grade-level content.

Identify Student Strengths: Prior to this activity, identify students' strengths and growth points by using the "Multiplying Decimal Fractions" prompt (p. 224) or something similar. Use student strengths to connect to new learning.

Materials:

- Base-ten blocks, KP® Ten-Frame Tiles, or other base-ten manipulatives
- Dry-erase boards and markers or paper and pencils
- Laminated sheets of graph paper for sketching (*optional*)

Create Pathways:

Launch

1. Pose the following scenario: James has 2 same-sized toys. Each weighs 6 pounds. How many pounds is that altogether?
2. Instruct students to sketch what this might look like.
3. Have students compare sketches to ensure everyone has an accurate sketch.

Explore

1. Divide students into pairs.
2. Have students work within their pairs using manipulatives, sketches, or numbers to show their work for the following scenario: James has 2 more same-sized toys, and each weighs 0.6 pounds. How many pounds is that altogether? (solution = 1.2 pounds)
3. As pairs finish, pose a new scenario: James has 2 more teeny-tiny same-sized toys, and each weighs 0.06 pounds. How much of a pound is that altogether? (solution = 0.12 pounds)

Discuss

1. Have students share their work with the group.
2. Ask prompting and probing questions to clarify their understanding of what they just did.

3. Write the following multiplication equations to help students look for a pattern: $2 \times 6 = 12$; $2 \times 0.6 = 1.2$; $2 \times 0.06 = 0.12$.

4. Ask students what they notice within and between the equations.

Wrap Up

1. **Check for Understanding:** Ask students to sketch 3×4. Next, ask students to sketch 3×0.4. Finally, ask students to sketch 3×0.04. Ask students to describe and explain the pattern that emerges.

2. **Connect to Grade-Level Content:** Explicitly connect multiplying decimal fractions to your current grade-level content, during both small group and whole-class time.

YOUR TURN

Throughout this chapter, you had the chance to view math small groups through the lens of the Math Small Group Framework. You focused on the math in the Fraction and Decimal Connections standards, looking at ways to identify strengths and planning for learning pathways. Now it's your turn. Take a moment to reflect on the questions that follow, focusing on how math small groups will benefit the teaching and learning in your classroom.

Learning Intention

After reading this chapter, you will understand how to target the math, identify strengths, and plan pathways for content related to Fraction and Decimal Connections.

Success Criteria

You will be able to use the math content trajectory for Fraction and Decimal Connections, in addition to your State Standards Framework or the *Math Small Group* Standards Trajectory Document, to help you identify the just-right starting place for your students.

The *Math Small Group* Standards Trajectory Document offers a map that shows how all the standards for each domain interrelate. To download this tool, visit resources.corwin.com/mathsmallgroups.

What ideas did you glean from this chapter that will help you engage in the three steps of the Math Small Group Framework?

What did you learn about the pathway of Fraction and Decimal Connections across grade levels? How will this help you as you work with your students in the math small group setting?

FINAL WORDS

Hello *again*, my friend!

You made it to the end! Whether you read this book cover to cover or hopped around to the topics that were most relevant to you, my hope is that you found what you were looking for to successfully set up your teacher-facilitated math small groups. This may have been your first introduction to math small group instruction, or you may have engaged in a review of great ideas you have been trying for years. Either way, I sincerely hope you found ways to enhance teaching and learning in your classroom.

In the first part of the book, we journeyed through a plethora of questions for getting started with small groups. We touched on everything from the "why" of math small group instruction to math small group membership to setting up your classroom to focusing on the math as a way to support students and provide access to all.

In the second part of the book, you had the chance to examine and apply the Math Small Group Framework through the lens of many different math topics. Throughout, my goal was to provide examples for how you target the math while supporting your students. By identifying and building on your students' strengths, you dramatically increase the probability that they will make meaningful and long-lasting connections.

And why is this work so important? For me, it has everything to do with the world in which our students are thriving. We live in a culture where it's okay to say and believe, "I'm not good at math." In fact, adults all around us often consider this something to brag and joke about. You know what I mean—jokes about being bad at math are all over our TV and movie screens. We need to do better by the next generation. We need to prepare them for a world where they confidently use mathematics as a set of tools to describe the world around them and problem-solve a multitude of situations. We owe them nothing less.

So, I leave you now with a renewed sense of how to help your students make sense of mathematics so they can describe and solve problems in the world around them. The implementation of math small groups provides you with a structure for supporting your students on their journey toward a math literate future.

Sincerely, and always for the kids,

Kimberly Rimbey

Kimberly Rimbey, PhD
National Board-Certified Teacher
Innovator and Encourager

APPENDIX A

Tips for Coaches and Leaders

This chapter is a bit different from the rest. Up until now, we've engaged in a conversation about how to set up teacher-facilitated math small groups, a conversation from the perspective of "we" as teachers. Because this final chapter focuses on the organizational infrastructure needed to support math small groups, I'm going to change my voice, speaking to you from the perspective of one coach offering support to another coach or instructional leader whose school is just beginning this work. Please note that if you are a building or organizational leader, this is every bit as relevant to you.

GETTING STARTED

I'm so excited that you're beginning this journey to support your teachers in designing a teacher-facilitated math small group model! There are so many things for you to think about as you get this work started. Please note that as I share from my experiences, we need to acknowledge that every context is different. Glean what you find helpful, and then make the process your own.

Start Small

I recommend limiting your scope at first, beginning work either with a single teacher or a single grade-level team. My personal preference is to focus on one grade level whenever possible. This allows teachers to collaborate when their Professional Learning Communities (PLCs) meet, troubleshoot when I am (you are) not around to coach, and build collegial professional bonds with another. It also supports buy-in to an emerging system we can refine and then share with other grade levels.

Initial Reflection

As your starting place, I encourage you to think about your "why." Why do you want to begin this journey of implementing teacher-facilitated math small groups? There are many other "how" questions to contemplate, but the "why" question needs to be your starting place. Here are some initial questions to help you refine your why:

- What is it about your student population that is leading you to consider implementing teacher-facilitated math small groups?

- What is it about your typical teacher profile that makes you want to go down this pathway?
- What do you hope to achieve through the implementation of teacher-facilitated math small groups?

Once you've articulated your "why," go ahead and shift to the other questions that naturally come to mind. Here are a few questions you might consider. Contemplating these questions ahead of time will help you navigate the conversations that come next.

- What are our goals?
- What outcomes do we want?
- What are the benefits?
- What are the costs?
- How will we know when we have been successful?
- How will we support our teachers in implementing teacher-facilitated math small groups?
- Who should be involved?
- Who are our stakeholders, and what will they need?
- How does this work fit with our school-wide goals, initiatives, and efforts?

Conversation With Leadership

Once you've reflected on the initial questions, the next step is to talk with other leaders to be sure this new structure will fit within their vision and instructional goals. Although you may want to chat with teachers ahead of time, it sometimes helps to be able to tell them that the leadership team is already on board. That said, your situation might lend itself to getting the teachers on board ahead of time and then going in as a team to talk with your building administrator. You know your situation best, so go with what your gut tells you.

For example, when talking with my principal about new ideas, I try to keep these conversations as open-ended as possible. Here's a sample of what one of my initial conversations might sound like:

- First, I share the school goal, initiative, or effort that I'm trying to connect to and ask my principal how she sees us moving toward that goal.
- Next, when the opportunity arises, I *briefly* describe my proposal with as few details as possible, connecting back to the relevant school or district goal, initiative, or effort. I check in to see what she thinks about that and if she's interested in hearing more.
- Then I let the conversation flow naturally, sharing my initial reflections as they are relevant. I also listen closely, ready to adjust my initial ideas based on what my principal says. I keep in mind that my initial reflections only represent my perspective, and I let my ideas morph in the moment.

- Near the end of the conversation, I ask if we can talk about next steps, careful to indicate that I'm willing to take on ownership of this project. I need my principal's blessing, and I let her know that I'm happy to involve her as much or as little as suits her.

When the conversation is finished, I recommend going back to your notes from the initial reflection and adjust them based on this conversation. You want to be sure you capture the emerging vision, which will be most successful if it's a shared vision.

CREATING THE INITIAL PLAN

Initial Reflection

Using Chapters 1–6 in this book, carefully design the math small groups plan. As with the conversation you have with leadership, you'll benefit tremendously if you deeply consider the work beforehand, anticipating how it will play out and what questions may come up.

Here are some of the questions to consider:

- What will success look like six months from now? One year from now? Five years from now?
- What do teachers need to know and be able to do to be successful?
- How can I best support teachers with unwrapping standards and establishing learning targets?
- How might we use the *Math Small Group* Standards Trajectory Document (or something similar) to identify unfinished learning from previous grades?
- How might we use the Deconstructing Standards Planning Template (or something similar) to clearly establish learning goals that are connected to the current grade-level learning goals?
- How might we use the Explore Before Explain Lesson Planning Template (or something similar) to plan teacher-facilitated math small groups?
- How will our teacher-facilitated math small group plan interface with heterogeneous whole group instruction (e.g., Liljedahl, 2021) and heterogeneous small group instruction (e.g., Dixon et al., 2019)?
- How will we ensure that the teacher-facilitated math small groups remain flexible and fluid, with students moving in and out of the groups once they have achieved access to the current grade-level math content?
- How will we use data to inform this endeavor?
- How will we coach teachers to collect and analyze data at all levels (checks for understanding, formative data, summative data, program data, etc.)?

Collaborative Design

Next, you'll want to set up a time to meet with the teachers who have agreed to participate. I recommend that you ask them to complete the Math Content Trajectory Reflection Questions (or something similar) to identify teaching strengths the team can lean into. Discuss these strengths as a team prior to diving into the teacher-facilitated math small groups conversation. The whole point to the pre-conversation is to drive the idea that good teaching is good teaching is good teaching. There should be direct connections between whole group instruction and what they do during the math small group sessions. Identifying their teaching strengths and opportunities for growth play a major role in the success of this work.

As with the leadership conversation, start by asking questions similar to those just listed. Be open to the teachers' responses, taking note of ways you might support and develop them, leaning into their teaching strengths as you collaboratively co-design the teacher-facilitated math small group systems and procedures. The goal of this conversation is to create an action plan for how you will use the tools to create your teacher-facilitated math small group system and procedures, including a timeline.

School-Wide Math Agreements

At the site level, bring teachers together within and across grades to determine school-wide agreements regarding common vocabulary, representations, symbols, processes, and the like. You can learn more about this process by referencing *The Math Pact, Elementary* by Karp et al. (2021).

> Check out *The Math Pact, Elementary* by Karp et al. (2021) and "13 Rules That Expire" by Karp et al. (2014).

Rapid-Cycle Iterative Design

The Plan-Do-Study-Act (PDSA) cycle is a useful model for guiding the development of a new system (see Figure A.1). I recommend you use the PDSA model (or something like it) to guide the team's work in the beginning stages. First, you'll create an implementation plan for the new model (Plan), described earlier, which you'll do during team meetings. Then you will carry out that plan (Do), observing and learning from the successes and challenges (Study). Finally, you and your teachers will determine how to modify the original plan, adjusting it accordingly (Act). As you continue the work, follow the PDSA cycle repeatedly until all the bugs are worked out.

Figure A.1 • *The Plan-Do-Study-Act Cycle*

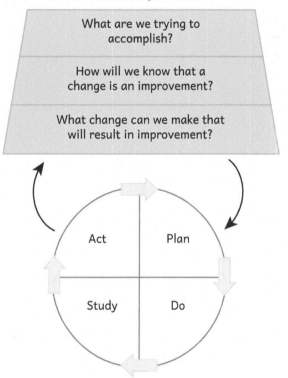

Source: Langley, Moen, Nolan K, et al. (2009).

Coaching Cycles

When I'm co-designing new systems with teachers, I find it helpful to include the coaching cycle as part of the conversation. Generally speaking, the coaching cycle includes three steps: precoaching planning, coaching session, and postcoaching reflection. It's important to note that the coaching session may include a plethora of strategies. Some of my favorites include co-teaching, demonstration teaching, whisper coaching, and side-by-side coaching. Although coaching models usually include observation and feedback as a viable strategy, I reserve pure observation and feedback for specific cases since it is less likely to develop teachers as thoroughly as some of the other strategies.

> Two great resources for learning more about the coaching cycle and specific coaching moves are Diane Sweeney's *Student-Centered Coaching: The Moves* (Sweeney & Harris, 2017) and *Leading Student-Centered Coaching: Building Principal and Coach Partnerships* (Sweeney & Mausbach, 2018).

Learning Lab

Over the years, I've innovated on the typical coaching moves and played with different formats. One format I find especially powerful includes setting up a Learning Lab. A Learning Lab is a classroom designed for co-teaching. Teachers bring their entire class with them to the Learning Lab, usually once per week, where we co-teach a preplanned lesson. I tend to plan with grade levels rather than with individual teachers, so we co-plan a co-teaching lesson, and each teacher brings their class to the Learning Lab the following week to implement our co-planned lesson.

I find this to be a powerful tool on many levels: the team dynamic provides for rich conversations, the teachers love that I prep our co-taught Learning Lab lessons, I can customize the learning episodes based on teacher strengths and growth trajectories, and the students love coming to the Learning Lab. Honestly, it's one of the most powerful teacher development tools I've designed. A Learning Lab would make a great place to experiment with teacher-facilitated math small groups as well. Of course, I still visit teachers in their classrooms, too. It's just nice to have a controlled environment to carry out our teaching experiments. Naturally, your teachers will need to meet with their teacher-facilitated math small groups every day, not just on the days when they're in the Learning Lab.

Math Small Group Meeting Space

In his book *Building Thinking Classrooms in Mathematics, Grades K–12*, Peter Liljedahl (2021) promotes rethinking the classroom space by providing students with opportunities to learn while standing. "Just because sitting and writing in a notebook is the obvious place for *some* activities, it does not have to be the workspace for *all* activities" (p. 58). I think this goes for the math small group format as well. I propose that we try letting students stand while we introduce the math small group task to them and then give them the option to sit or stand while working on it. I always have clipboards on hand, so they could certainly use those. They could even choose to sit on the floor to work. It simply means I need to rethink the space where the math small group is meeting. This might be a great experiment for the Learning Lab setting. And while we're at it, perhaps we might try out Liljedahl's suggestion for using vertical non-permanent surfaces (VNPS) as well (pp. 56–68). Liljedahl's research revealed that when using VNPS, students are more willing to take risks, revise their thinking, and learn from each other.

Communication Is Key

If your site or organizational leaders have given you the go-ahead to run with the teacher-facilitated math small groups model, be sure to keep them in the loop. In my experience, leaders love to hear about both successes and challenges and how we're monitoring and adjusting along the way.

SCALING UP

Scaling Up Across a School

Once you've designed a model that works, you're probably going to find that word spreads throughout the school. When I first started my Learning Lab, I invited only the teachers who had expressed interest. Within just a couple of weeks, teachers all over campus were asking if they could bring their classes to the Learning Lab, too. The same will happen with your teacher-facilitated math small groups. Once you and the teachers start experiencing success, word is going to spread. And then other teachers and grade levels will start asking if they can replicate what you're doing.

When this starts happening, go with it. I recommend that at that point, you revisit the process you used for the original collaborative design and plan a similar process for other teams or grade levels. It may be abbreviated because you will have already designed the system, but the initial reflection and conversation are important to the onboarding process.

Scaling Up Across a District

In my experience, once a school has found success with a system such as teacher-facilitated math small groups, word starts spreading across campuses as well. If leaders from other schools begin inquiring, go with it and start talking to them about how they might bring the teacher-facilitated math small groups model to their schools. That said, if this does not happen organically, you can start planting seeds by talking with the coaches and/or site leaders at the other campuses, emphasizing the success found when addressing unfinished learning by connecting it to grade-level expectations. After all, we all want to help our students succeed, right?

Either way, keep in mind that as this model moves from one school to the next, it may take on a new flavor that works for that campus. Don't be afraid to let them experiment, just as the initial group did. Recommend that they start small and embed the PDSA cycle into their work, just as was done at the original school.

APPENDIX B

Sources on Topics Related to Math Small Groups

ASSESSMENT AND ANALYSIS RESOURCES

Ashlock, R. B. (2006). *Error patterns in computation: Using error patterns to improve instruction* (9th ed.). Pearson.

Bamburger, H. J., Oberdorf, C., & Schultz-Ferrell, K. (2009). *Math misconceptions: From misunderstanding to deep understanding*. Heinemann.

Keeley, P., & Tobey, C. R. (2011). *Mathematics formative assessment: 75 practical strategies for linking assessment, instruction, and learning*. Corwin.

Newton, N. (2016). *Math running records in action: A framework for assessing basic fact fluency in grades K–5*. Routledge.

PLANNING AND PREPARATION FOR TEACHER-FACILITATED MATH SMALL GROUP INSTRUCTION RESOURCES

Almarode, J., Fisher, D., Thunder, K., & Frey, N. (2021). *The success criteria playbook: A hands-on guide to making learning visible and measurable*. Corwin.

Fisher, D., Frey, N., & Smith, D. (2020). *The teacher credibility and collective efficacy playbook*. Corwin.

Hattie, J., Fisher, D., & Frey, N. (2017). *Visible Learning for mathematics: What works best to optimize student learning*. Corwin.

Karp, K. S., Dougherty, B. J., & Bush, S. B. (2021). *The math pact, elementary: Achieving instructional coherence within and across grades*. Corwin.

Kobett, B. M., & Karp, K. S. (2020). *Strengths-based teaching and learning in mathematics: Teaching turnarounds for grades K–6*. Corwin.

Liljedahl, P. (2021). *Building thinking classrooms in mathematics, grades K–12: 14 teaching practices for enhancing learning*. Corwin.

Moore, S., & Rimbey, K. (2021). *Mastering math manipulatives: Concrete and virtual representations*. Corwin.

Nagro, S., Daley, J., & Gaspard, C. (2019). UDL in mathematics. In W. W. Murawski & K. L. Scott (Eds.), *What really works with universal design for learning* (pp. 35–63). Corwin.

National Council of Teachers of Mathematics. (2014). *Principles to actions: Ensuring mathematical success for all*. Author.

National Council of Teachers of Mathematics. (2020). *Catalyzing change in early childhood and elementary mathematics*. Author.

Sullivan, P., & Lilburn, P. (2002). *Good questions for math teaching: Why ask them and what to ask, K–6*. Math Solutions Publications.

Zager, T. J. (2017). *Becoming the math teacher you wish you'd had: Ideas and strategies from vibrant classrooms*. Stenhouse.

SMALL GROUP INTERACTIONS AND ACTIVITIES TO USE WITH MATH SMALL GROUPS

Dick, L., White, T. F., Trocki, A., Sztajn, P., Heck, D., & Herrema, K. (2016). Supporting sense making with mathematical bet lines. *Teaching Children Mathematics, 22*(9), 538–545. https://www.nctm.org/Publications/Teaching-Children-Mathematics/2016/Vol22/Issue9/TCM2016_05_538a/

Franke, M. L., Kazemi, E., & Turrou, A. C. (2018). *Choral counting and counting collections: Transforming the preK–5 math classroom*. Stenhouse.

McCoy, A., Barnett, J., & Combs, E. (2013). *High-yield routines*. National Council of Teachers of Mathematics.

Muson, J. (2018). *In the moment: Conferring in the elementary classroom*. Heinemann.

Wedekind, K. O. (2011). *Math exchanges: Guiding young mathematicians in small-group meetings*. Stenhouse.

West, L. (2018). *Adding talk to the equation: A self-study guide for teachers and coaches on improving math discussions*. Stenhouse.

CENTERS, WORK STATIONS, AND ACTIVITIES FOR THE WHOLE CLASS RESOURCES

Diller, D. (2011). *Math work stations: Independent learning you can count on, K–2*. Stenhouse.

Newton, N. (2013). *Guided math in action: Building each student's mathematical proficiency with small-group instruction*. Routledge.

Newton, N. (2016). *Math workshop in action: Strategies for grades K–5*. Routledge.

Sammons, L. (2010). *Guided math: A framework for mathematics instruction*. Huntington Shell Education.

Sammons, L., & Boucher, D. (2017). *Guided math workshop*. Huntington Shell Education.

Siena, M. (2009). *From reading to math: How best practices in literacy can make you a better math teacher, grades K–5*. Math Solutions Publications.

MULTITIER SYSTEMS OF SUPPORT AND RTI RESOURCES

Buffum, A., Mattos, M., & Malone, J. (2018). *Taking action: A handbook for RTI at Work™*. Solution Tree.

Hall, S. L. (2018). *10 success factors for literacy intervention: Getting results with MTSS in elementary schools*. Association of Supervision and Curriculum Development.

Kanold, T. D., Schuhl, S., Larson, M. R., Barnes, B., Kanold-McIntyre, J., & Toncheff, M. (2018). *Mathematics assessment and intervention in a PLC at Work®*. Solution Tree.

REFERENCES

Ashlock, R. B. (2006). *Error patterns in computation: Using error patterns to improve instruction* (9th ed.). Pearson.

Bay-Williams, J. M., & SanGiovanni, J. J. (2021). *Figuring out fluency in mathematics teaching and learning, grades K–8: Moving beyond basic facts and memorization.* Corwin.

Brown, P. (2019, July). Explore-before-explain. *Science and Children, 56*(9), 38–43.

CAST. (2018). The UDL guidelines. https://udlguidelines.cast.org

Chardin, M., & Novak, K. (2021). *Equity by design: Delivering on the power and promise of UDL.* Corwin.

Dick, L., White, T. F., Trocki, A., Sztajn, P., Heck, D., & Herrema, K. (2016). Supporting sense making with mathematical bet lines. *Teaching Children Mathematics, 22*(9), 538–545. https://www.nctm.org/Publications/Teaching-Children-Mathematics/2016/Vol22/Issue9/TCM2016_05_538a/

Diller, D. (2011). *Math work stations: Independent learning you can count on, K–2.* Stenhouse Publishers.

Dixon, J. K., Brooks, L. A., & Carli, M. R. (2019). *Making sense of mathematics for teaching: The small group.* Solution Tree.

Hattie, J., Fisher, D., & Frey, N. (2017). *Visible learning for mathematics: What works best to optimize student learning.* Corwin.

Hoffer, W. W. (2012). *Minds on mathematics: Using math workshop to develop deep understanding in grades 4–8.* Heinemann.

Karp, K. S., Bush, S. B., & Dougherty, B. J. (2014). 13 rules that expire. *Teaching Children Mathematics, 21*(1), 18–25.

Karp, K. S., Dougherty, B. J., & Bush, S. B. (2021). *The math pact, elementary: Achieving instructional coherence within and across grades.* Corwin.

Keeley, P., & Tobey, C. R. (2011). *Mathematics formative assessment: 75 practical strategies for linking assessment, instruction, and learning.* Corwin.

Kobett, B. M., & Karp, K. S. (2020). *Strengths-based teaching and learning in mathematics: Teaching turnarounds for grades K–6.* Corwin.

Leinwand, S. (2022, February 14). *Practical approaches for providing school and district leadership that strengthens mathematics teaching and learning.* Arizona Mathematics Leaders Annual Conference, Phoenix.

Lesh, R. A., Post, T., & Behr, M. (1987). Representations and translations among representations in mathematics learning and problem solving. In C. Janvier (Ed.), *Problems of representations in the teaching and learning of mathematics* (pp. 33–40). Lawrence Erlbaum. http://www.cehd.umn.edu/ci/rationalnumberproject/87_5.html

Liljedahl, P. (2021). *Building thinking classrooms in mathematics, grades K–12: 14 teaching practices for enhancing learning.* Corwin.

Moore, S., & Rimbey, K. (2021). *Mastering math manipulatives: Concrete and virtual representations.* Corwin.

Moore, S., & Rimbey, K. (2022). *Mastering math manipulatives: Hands-on and virtual activities for building and connecting mathematical ideas.* Corwin.

National Council of Teachers of Mathematics. (2014). *Principles to actions: Ensuring mathematical success for all.* Author.

National Council of Teachers of Mathematics. (2020). *Catalyzing change in early childhood and elementary mathematics.* Author.

Newton, N. (2013). *Guided math in action: Building each student's mathematical proficiency with small-group instruction.* Routledge.

Newton, N. (2016a). *Math running records in action: A framework for assessing basic fact fluency in grades K–5.* Routledge.

Newton, N. (2016b). *Math workshop in action: Strategies for grades K–5.* Routledge.

Sammons, L. (2010). *Guided math: A framework for mathematics instruction.* Huntington Shell Education.

Sammons, L., & Boucher, D. (2017). *Guided math workshop.* Shell Education.

SanGiovanni, J. J., Katt, S., & Dykema, K. J. (2020). *Productive math struggle:*

A 6-point action plan for fostering perseverance. Corwin.

Sweeney, D., & Harris, L. A. (2017). *Student-centered coaching: The moves.* Corwin.

Sweeney, D., & Mausbach, A. (2018). *Leading student-centered coaching: Building principal and coach partnerships.* Corwin.

INDEX

Figures and objects are indicated by f after the page number.

Supporting TEACHERS | Empowering STUDENTS

NOW AVAILABLE: Supplement to modify the practices for different settings

PETER LILJEDAHL

14 optimal practices for thinking that create an ideal setting for deep mathematics learning to occur

Grades K–12

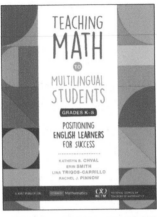

KATHRYN B. CHVAL, ERIN SMITH, LINA TRIGOS-CARRILLO, RACHEL J. PINNOW

Strengths-based approaches to support multilingual students' development in mathematics

Grades K–8

HILARY KREISBERG, MATTHEW L. BEYRANEVAND

Guidance on building productive relationships with families about math education

Grades K–5

BETH MCCORD KOBETT, FRANCIS (SKIP) FENNELL, KAREN S. KARP, DELISE ANDREWS, LATRENDA KNIGHTEN, JEFF SHIH, DESIREE HARRISON, BARBARA ANN SWARTZ, SORSHA-MARIA T. MULROE

Detailed plans for helping elementary students experience deep mathematical learning

Grades K–1, 2–3, 4–5

BETH MCCORD KOBETT, KAREN S. KARP

Your game plan for unlocking mathematics by focusing on students' strengths

Grades K–6

JOHN J. SANGIOVANNI, SUSIE KATT, KEVIN J. DYKEMA

A guide for empowering students to embrace productive struggle to build essential skills for learning and living—both inside and outside the classroom

Grades K–12

To order, visit corwin.com/math